efore the

JENNY LIND

BOOKS BY EDWARD WAGENKNECHT

Jenny Lind

JENNY LIND

BY
EDWARD WAGENKNECHT

With Illustrations

Boston and New York
HOUGHTON MIFFLIN COMPANY
The Riverside Press Cambridge

The Riverside Press
CAMBRIDGE · MASSACHUSETTS
PRINTED IN THE U.S.A.

TO MY FRIENDS
DR. AND MRS. FREDERICK ADAMS

... Biography has often been allotted to writers who seem very little acquainted with the nature of their task, or very negligent about the performance. They rarely afford any other account than might be collected from public papers, but imagine themselves to be writing a life when they exhibit a chronological series of actions or preferments; and so little regard the manners or behavior of their heroes, that more knowledge may be gained of a man's real character, by a short conversation with one of his servants, than from a formal and studied narrative, begun with his pedigree, and ended with his funeral.

SAMUEL JOHNSON: *The Rambler*

... The first and perhaps the only duty of an honest biographer is, so far as may be, to set forth the man of whom he writes as that man saw himself, and to explain him on his own terms.

BARRETT WENDELL

To define an individuality, to sublimate the essence of a personality, is the prime reason for putting a man or a woman on paper, whether it be in actual biography, or in the imaginary biography which is fiction.

WINNIFRED KING RUGG: *Unafraid*

It is a great mistake to think that people's characters alter as they grow older; though different circumstances may bring different sides of them into prominence.

LORD DAVID CECIL: *The Stricken Deer*

PREFACE

MISS WILLA CATHER has argued that, in order to impart true feeling to a novel or a story, the writer thereof must have known the material which he employs in childhood, long before he had any idea of using it in a work of art. All the stuff of her own fictions, she tells us, was gathered together before she was twenty: since then she has only been recollecting and reassembling.

I do not know whether Miss Cather would extend her remarks to include biographical writing or not, but it seems to me that the principle might be made to apply, in a limited way, in this field. My maternal grandfather, Henry Erichsen, was a sailor on the Atlantic in the days of the clipper-ships. Though he was not a man with any particular interest in the arts, somewhere and somehow he happened to hear Jenny Lind. She made a profound impression upon him and he cherished her memory all his life. Whenever singing or singers were mentioned in his presence thereafter, he would exclaim, 'Ah! but you ought to have heard Jenny Lind!' And the implication was, clearly, that there was nothing more to be said.

His enthusiasm became a tradition in the family, and Jenny Lind was always for us, *par excellence*, the singer. It was thus that I first heard her name, and I believe this faint point of contact, this early appreciation of the typical attitude of her contemporary admirers toward her, has helped me not inconsiderably in drawing the lines of this portrait. Indeed, it seems to me extremely doubtful whether I should ever have been drawn to Jenny Lind as subject, had it not been for this circumstance. So far as one can tell about such things, it may be said that my sailor-grandfather's enthusiasm was the real begetter of this book.

Of course, he taught me nothing about Jenny Lind save the bare fact that she was a singer. For many years her outlines were vague and shadowy in my mind, like those of a legend. And here I think I did not differ greatly from the vast body of my contemporaries. Today the echo of Jenny's fame has reached almost every one, yet there are surprisingly few who really know anything about her.

For this state of affairs there are several good reasons. Her authorized biography — the work of Henry Scott Holland and W. S. Rockstro — has long been out of print. Though in many

respects an admirable piece of work, the book
has the limitations characteristic of authorized
biographies in the Victorian age — it was indeed dedicated to the Queen — and one could
hardly expect to find many readers for it today.
And except for the brief and unsympathetic
sketch in Mr. Werner's 'Barnum,' the modern
biographer has hitherto neglected Jenny Lind
entirely: the only book published about her in
recent years is the wholly uncritical record by
her daughter, Mrs. Raymond Maude.

Except those of C. G. Rosenberg and N.
Parker Willis, few of the strictly contemporary
writings on Jenny Lind have any particular interest or value for us today. Most of them are
either frank 'puffs' or else mere uncritical com-
pilations, and many of them are full of dreadful
inaccuracies. Like most things written about
theatrical celebrities while they are alive, these
books are not especially concerned with facts:
their whole interest is enlisted in creating a
legend. I know that all generalizations have
become notoriously unsafe, yet I suppose one
may still venture to say that of all the human
beings who have become the subject of legends,
none ever yet bore any very close resemblance
to the image that was created of him. The

George Washington legend crumbled some time ago. Recently the late Albert J. Beveridge performed an heroic pioneering service in demolishing some of the more obnoxious features of the Lincoln legend. In the theater, however, we still have many of our legends intact. Some, like the Bernard Shaw legend and the Mary Garden legend, are assiduously cultivated by the subjects themselves, through a zealous and untiring use of every device that the modern publicity expert knows. The Barrymores, on the other hand, have never needed to develop their own legend. Others obligingly do it for them: indeed, it has already enlisted the friendly offices of two gifted and accommodating playwrights.

In this book, I have attempted a study of Jenny Lind the woman, in her art life and in her personal life. My aim has been to show her as she was, so far as that can be accomplished at this date, without disparagement and without eulogy. The book contains no 'new,' in the sense of hitherto unpublished, material. It contains a good deal of new material, however, in the sense that many volumes of nineteenth-century reminiscence and biography are for the first time brought to bear upon the study of

Jenny Lind. Some of these books — for example, those connected with John Addington Symonds — are very important, and contain much more information about Jenny Lind than a good many of the writings devoted specifically to her.

This book is not a biography in the usual sense: it is a portrait, a psychograph. Its method is the psychographic method. Those interested in technical considerations, in the origin and development of psychography in the writings of Mr. Gamaliel Bradford, as well as in my own convictions concerning it, will find the matter rather fully adumbrated in the appendix to my book, 'The Man Charles Dickens: A Victorian Portrait,' which was published by Houghton Mifflin Company in 1929. In general, it seemed to the writer that that book was rather splendidly reviewed. There are some reviewers, however, who, in spite of the fact that Mr. Bradford has been both practicing and expounding psychography since 1912, and even though all modern biographical writing has been more or less influenced by his work, are still totally at sea concerning both the aims and the methods of the new craft. At one time, I intended a further discussion of the matter in

this place, but fuller reflection convinced me
that I had nothing to add to — and certainly
nothing to retract from — what I wrote in 1929.
So far as any supplementary consideration of
the matter is called for at this time, it will all be
found, by implication, in the four quotations
which I have placed at the beginning of the
book.

There remains to acknowledge, inadequately,
my obligations. To Mr. Bradford my indebtedness is, as always, greater than can be expressed.
Mr. Leonidas Westervelt, of Douglaston, Long
Island, I look upon as, in this instance, almost a
collaborator, since he has furnished all the illustrations in this volume from his magnificent
collection, and I am sure very many will find
his by far the most interesting part of the book.
Mr. W. A. Hildebrand, Dr. Johannes Hoving,
and Miss Kitty Cheatham, all of New York, are
other special students of Jenny Lind to whom I
am under no inconsiderable obligations. Officials of the New York Public Library, the Public Library of the City of Boston, the Harvard
College Library, and the Library of the University of Washington have all been unfailingly
helpful. Special thanks are due to Mr. H. M.
Lydenberg of the first institution named, as well

as to Mr. George P. Utley, who gave me unusual privileges at the Newberry Library in Chicago and thus made my work much easier than it would otherwise have been. Miss Geraldine Farrar helped me over some hard places, and Mr. M. R. Werner and Mr. and Mrs. L. Edward Scriven, of New York City, and Mr. Lawrence J. Zillman, of Seattle, have been kind in various ways. Finally, I wish to thank my publisher, Mr. Ferris Greenslet, who is responsible for the existence of the book in this form, and whose interest and encouragement during its preparation has been much more than the conventional sort.

EDWARD WAGENKNECHT

CONTENTS

ILLUSTRATIONS

Illustrations

All the illustrations are from the collection of Mr.
Leonidas Westervelt, of Douglaston, Long Island.

JENNY LIND

I
THE LEGEND

The youth of her day have borne her in their hearts across a generation, and their hearts still rise at the mention of her name, as the Garde du Roi sprang up cheering to their feet when the Queen appeared.

GEORGE WILLIAM CURTIS

JENNY LIND

∵

CHAPTER I

The Legend

I

THREE quarters of a century ago, our grandfathers went mad over a simple Swedish woman, quite without physical beauty, and aus-
terely disdainful toward most of the fetching
idiosyncrasies of the 'prima donna,' whom a
great museum *impresario* and self-styled professor of the art of 'humbug' had brought to the
United States for an extensive concert tour.

It was the first such tour ever undertaken by
a European celebrity, and it still remains the
most spectacular and successful of them all.
Like printing, the art of ballyhooing a singer
was born at a very high point of development,
and the name of its Johannes Gutenberg was
P. T. Barnum.

There were giants in those days, but they
shrank, all of them, beside Jenny Lind. In the

large cities, the box office was not good enough for her tickets: they must be sold at public auction. The record 'high' was reached in Boston, where the first ticket was purchased for six hundred and twenty-five dollars by a minor vocalist named Ossian F. Dodge. Now Jenny Lind herself was no business woman, and she understood the intimate New World connection between art and commerce as little as did the Music Master in the famous Belasco play. So when the news was conveyed to her, she expressed, with all her customary frankness, the opinion that Ossian F. Dodge was a fool.[1] But Dodge was not a fool: he was simply a good American. The next time he gave a concert he advertised it by means of a vivid poster which showed Barnum introducing him to Jenny Lind. He reaped his reward.[2]

Naturally it was quite hopeless for a mere poet and college professor, like Henry Wadsworth Longfellow, to compete in such a running: the best he could do was to spend eight dollars and content himself with a seat in the gallery.[3] But of course even eight dollars is a good deal of money, a fact recognized nowhere more clearly and more profitably than by the ingenious proprietor of a livery stable located

4

PHINEAS TAYLOR BARNUM

near the Boston concert hall. With him to realize was to act, and being a public-spirited man, he determined to provide a limited number of chairs at the extremely reasonable price of fifty cents each. These were located in his own place of business, and it is said that a fair number of Bostonians did not cavil to take up their stations in even so inappropriate an environment, hoping that if the wind were favorable, some at least of the divine melody might reach them there.[4]

This was by no means the most ridiculous incident of the tour. Indeed, there were times when the enthusiasm of the populace even reached the riot stage.[5] But I think the sweetest tribute of all was reserved for Providence, Rhode Island, where the thrifty chambermaid of the hotel where Jenny Lind was staying — she ought to have been related to Barnum — began lining her pockets with gold by the simple expedient of selling quantities of hair from her own blonde head to undesigning purchasers who were firmly persuaded that she had taken them from the great singer's brush.[6]

When Jenny Lind arrived in New York on the first of September, 1850, there were thirty thousand people out to meet the boat. Even

5

the gods were on Barnum's side: it was the
Sabbath; church services were over; nobody in
the city had anything in particular to do. In
the excitement several persons were injured,
and one man was swept off the dock into the
water. The crowd trailed along to the Irving
House, and by night Broadway was completely
blocked. Escorted by the Fire Department —
F. S. Chanfrau, in 'A Glance at New York,'
was then at the height of his glory — the New
York Musical Fund Society gave a concert in
her honor, and the programme did not termi-
nate until well past midnight. The performers
enjoyed the festivities greatly, but history does
not record the impressions of the guest of honor,
who was worn out from travelling, and spending her first night in a strange, vast country.

There was to be no privacy for Jenny Lind.
'Her rooms,' wrote Barnum later in his Autobiography, 'were thronged by visitors, including the magnates of the land in both Church
and State. The carriages of the wealthiest citizens could be seen in front of her hotel at nearly
all hours of the day, and it was with some difficulty that I prevented the "fashionables" from
monopolizing her altogether, and thus, as I believed, sadly marring my interests by cutting

6

her off from the warm sympathies she had awakened among the masses.'[7] He had no need to fear. No class was going to monopolize Jenny Lind. The manufacturers and the newspapers were taking care of that.

'Milliners, mantua-makers, and shopkeepers' besieged her, naming articles for her, presenting them to her, and begging the favor of an autograph in return. Barnum mentions Jenny Lind gloves, bonnets, riding-hats, shawls, mantillas, robes, chairs, sofas, pianos. Songs and poems were dedicated to her, and dances were named after her. Her name and her picture appeared on water carafes. Hotels served their choicest dishes *à la Jenny Lind*.[8] There was a Jenny Lind tea-kettle, 'which, being filled with water and placed on the fire, commences to *sing* in a few minutes.' In Lynn, Massachusetts, Jenny Lind sausages were placed on sale.[9] There was a Jenny Lind pancake,[10] and in far-away Alaska the time was coming when, in the days of the gold rush, a baker would nail out a shingle announcing that he made Jenny Lind cakes.[11] Though she loathed tobacco as Madame Jeritza loathes it today, there was a cigar named after her, and in Boston there was a 'Jenny Lind Hotel' which was nothing other than a common barroom.[12] At the same time, all sorts of fantastic stories were circulated about her. She had a curious, individual method of dressing her hair, massing its coils on each side of her head. From this circumstance arose the legend, which was widely believed, that she had no ears whatever.[13] All in all, few persons have ever been the object of more widespread curiosity.

And it was not only the tradesmen who had lost their heads. In Rensselaer County, New York, Jenny Lind was nominated for the Assembly. She received a vote for Lieutenant-Governor in Massachusetts, and in New York City several persons named her as their choice for Mayor. I don't know that anything has impressed me more as to the universality of her triumph than the fact that even the secluded and individualistic Emerson waxed enthusiastic in his praise of her.[14] George P. Upton wrote later that he could compare the ovation only with the famous reception of Kossuth and the magnificent welcome of General Grant and peace together at the close of the Civil War.[15]

Of course many Americans were deliberately going out of their way to vindicate the honor of Charles Dickens, proving beyond the shadow of a doubt that 'Martin Chuzzlewit' was an accur-

8

ate picture of American life. A New-Yorker who found one of Jenny Lind's gloves was said to have exhibited it publicly, charging one shilling to kiss the outside and two shillings to kiss the inside where her hand had been. The incident has distinctly a Chuzzlewitian flavor. And even if it should turn out to be apocryphal, there would still be the story of the shawl which Jenny dropped one day while standing on a balcony, and which, before it could be recovered, had been pounced upon by the thundering herd and torn to shreds for souvenirs.[16] At the first concert in Castle Garden, it was noted with some surprise that the men in the audience far outnumbered the women. The same thing was true at Boston. The ladies had been afraid to venture into the crush. Of those who did, many suffered serious discomfort; some had their clothes torn off their backs. In New York a group of enthusiasts and rowdies besieged the hall by boat from the Hudson River, and the police had to be called out to drive them away.[17]

And the newspapers! The morning after her arrival, and before she had sung a note on this side of the water, the 'New York Tribune' had four columns on the first page describing her reception, and a poem with fifty-two footnotes

9

explaining the Scandinavian allusions in it. Journalism was erudite in those days. The papers published a facsimile of the ticket to her concerts and listed the names of the purchasers.[18] In a special column, they reported from day to day the 'Movements of the Swedish Nightingale.' The 'New York Herald' found her appearance 'as significant an event as the appearance of Dante, Tasso, Raphael, Shakespeare, Goethe, Thorwaldsen, or Michael Angelo,' and hailed it as a sign 'that the wand of civilization has fallen from the hands of the southern nations and passed to the hardy northern races.' 'She has changed all men's ideas of music as much so as Bacon's inductive system revolutionized philosophy.' Again she was proclaimed 'the most popular woman in the world at this moment, — perhaps the most popular that ever was in it.' As for her warblings, they were described as things 'which she spins out from her throat like the attenuated fibre from the silkworm, dying away so sweetly and so gradually, till it seems melting into the song of the seraphim and is lost in eternity.' Which, it must be admitted, would be a great achievement for a silkworm, to say the least. When she returned to New York after her tour, one hys-

CASTLE GARDEN, NEW YORK

terical gentleman wrote: 'Jenny Lind is once
more among us — God bless her! — and we
wish we had a more deferential medium where-
with to announce her movements, for she
should scarcely be named but in a blessing or a
prayer.' [19] They are rather violent utterances to
be coming from responsible metropolitan dai-
lies in time of peace — are they not? [20]

II

Certainly it would seem to have been a suffi-
ciently exciting reception for a singer. For that
is what this woman was, and that is all she was.
She had not swum across the English Channel;
she had never crossed the Atlantic Ocean in a
flying machine; nor had she done anything else
that was sensational and spectacular — and
useless. She had not even, like her famous
contemporary, Lola Montez, been the mistress
of the King of Bavaria. She was simply a singer.

As a singer, she stands, even today, somewhat
in a world apart. There are other famous
musicians of the past — Malibran, Sontag,
Grisi, Alboni, Campanini — what are they but
names? Even Patti and Tamagno are already
receding definitely in the memory of human-
kind. But Jenny Lind? That is another story.

11

She is more than a name: she is a presence, a fragrance. If she suggests nothing else, she suggests the romance of the past, the pathos of distance. She is the best-known singer of other days, but she is more than that: she is actually better known than many a singer who is thriving today. There is a caressing something about the very name of her, and it is spoken and heard even now with an impulse of tenderness. Occasionally, to be sure, you find a man like Charles T. Congdon who looks back upon his youthful enthusiasm for her with an impulse of disgust: 'I only wish that I had my dozen dollars safe again in my purse, that I might spend them in buying old books, or in securing tickets for the next Philharmonic series.' [21] But much more typical, infinitely more characteristic are the gallant words of George William Curtis, quoted at the beginning of this chapter. Ridiculous as the Jenny Lind craze was, disgusting as it was in some of its manifestations, the fact remains that this woman captivated the imagination of her century as no other artist had done it, and that though her art is as dead now as the snows of yesterday, she still holds something of her old charm for us who look back at her through the gathering mists of time.

12

The American visit was, of course, simply a brief interlude in a long musical career. In Europe her admirers habitually employed somewhat less rowdy methods of manifesting their enthusiasm, but the enthusiasm was there just the same. And no more than with us was it confined to the upper classes: it filtered down through the strata of society until her name had become a household word to thousands who had never heard her voice. England, indeed, had anticipated a good many of our tricks. Cigars were named for her there as well as here, and servants' caps and melons and flies for trout-fishing.[22] An early biographer records that one royal admirer, whose ingenuity was more commendable than his taste, had sent her a golden goblet filled with ants' eggs — the food of nightingales; also that Queen Victoria had presented her 'with a superb nightingale, manufactured entirely of precious gems, which she wore in her hair, and acknowledged with a graceful smile and a happy gesture toward the royal box.'[23] In Germany, one paper had compared her singing to that of the archangels around the throne of the Almighty.[24] Remembering that in our own day, Mr. Edward Moore, the companionable critic of the 'Chicago Tribune,' once accused Mr. Tito Schipa of singing like 'a young tenor angel,' one is tempted to pause a moment and to wonder where these musicians get their intimate knowledge of celestial things. Perhaps, after all, Abt Vogler was right:

The rest may reason and welcome: 'tis we musicians know.

The great composers, the artists, the poets of Europe had accepted Jenny Lind as their peer. Queen Victoria — Victorianism incarnate — had officially placed the sanction of the age upon her. And even Disraeli, whom we do not usually think of as a sentimentalist, had said of her career as artist and philanthropist that it almost reached 'the high ideal of human nature.' [25]

What was even more striking was the attitude of the various churches. Those were the days when most of the godly sensed at least a faint odor of brimstone whenever they passed the doors of a theater. Yet, when Jenny Lind set out on her tour of the English provinces, the Bishop of Norwich invited her to make the episcopal palace her headquarters during her stay in the city. One may not say that the invitation passed unchallenged. A religious journal commented: 'It is very right and proper

CATCHING THE SWEDISH NIGHTINGALE

that jackdaws should build in the church. They have vested interests there. But farewell to the primitive purity of the establishment when it affords a resting-place to nightingales.' [26] But the invitation was a splendid and a daring tribute, nevertheless, and the wonder is that it excited so little comment.

In America, too, there were pious persons who did not accept her. One was the crazy woman who in 1850, in New York, published the scurrilous pamphlet known as 'Mahomet; or the Unveiled Prophet of Inistan: A Bouquet for Jenny Lind.' [27] Another was a lady whom Samuel Scoville, Jr., has only recently rescued from oblivion in one of his delightful essays, Mrs. Niles Wadsworth, wife of the village blacksmith of Cornwall, Connecticut. 'When Barnum brought Jennie Lind to New York, Niles planned to travel down and hear her. If he went to hear a play actress, his wife warned him, she would never speak to him again. He did and she didn't. They lived together after that for over twenty years, but she never spoke a word to him from that day on, even when he lay a-dying.' [28] But much more representative of the general point of view is the well-known anecdote of Father Taylor, the famous preacher of the Seamen's Bethel in Boston, which has often been told, but deserves to be told again. Father Taylor was opposed to dancing, theater-going, and card-playing, but he had a passionate love for music. One day when, all unaware of Jenny Lind's presence in the audience, he was in the midst of a warm tribute to her talents and her many virtues, a long, lank individual rose up on the steps of the pulpit and asked him whether a person who died at one of Miss Lind's concerts would go to heaven. The preacher glared at him disgustedly as he replied, 'A Christian will go to heaven wherever he dies; and a fool will be a fool wherever he is — even if he is on the steps of the pulpit.' [29]

III

Johanna Maria Lind was born in Stockholm, Sweden, on October 6, 1820. The family was poor. For reasons which it is not necessary to go into here, the baby did not fit well into the life of the household, and as soon as she could be separated from her mother, she was placed in the care of Carl Ferndal, organist of the parish church at Ed-Sollentua, fifteen miles from Stockholm.

In 1829, when Jenny was only nine years old,

16

her voice was discovered by one Mlle. Lundberg, a dancer at the Royal Opera House, whose maid had chanced to hear the child singing to her cat. The dancer was fortunate enough to enlist the interest of Herr Croelius, Court-Secretary and Singing-Master at the Royal Theater, through whom Jenny was introduced to Count Puke, and entered as a pupil in the theater-school, to be trained as a singer and an actress.

Her first appearance on the stage occurred in 1830, in a melodrama called 'The Polish Mine.' Technically, her operatic début took place in 1836, when she appeared as Georgette in a forgotten Swedish opera by Lindblad, 'Frondörene,' but this was of small importance and attracted little attention, and Jenny's real début did not come until March 7, 1838, when she appeared as Agatha in 'Der Freischütz.' Thenceforth, as Bernard Shaw would say, she became a person with some business in the world.

Jenny Lind remained in Stockholm until 1841 when, becoming dissatisfied with her progress, she reluctantly journeyed to Paris, to seek the instruction of Manuel Garcia. Garcia, centenarian, brother of Malibran and Viardot, inventor of the laryngoscope, was possibly the

17

greatest singing-teacher who ever lived. In any case, it was he who taught Jenny Lind what singing is, in the technical sense, and from this time on, her progress was rapid. Enlisting the good will of Meyerbeer, she appeared in Berlin, as Norma, on December 15, 1844, with triumphant success. On April 22, 1846, she made her Viennese début in the same character; and a little more than a month later, she created a tremendous sensation when she appeared as featured soloist at the Lower Rhine Music Festival at Aix-la-Chapelle, singing both in Haydn's 'Creation' and in Händel's 'Alexander's Feast.' She appeared for the first time in London, on May 4, 1847, at Her Majesty's Theater, as Alice in 'Roberto il Diavolo,' and her farewell to opera was sung at the same theater and in the same character, almost exactly two years later — May 10, 1849.

Meanwhile, she had begun to identify herself with oratorio, with which her name was so long to be associated in England, and which was to win her a unique place in the heart of the nation. On December 15, 1848, she had sung in London in Mendelssohn's 'Elijah'; now, August 19, 1850, she established her supremacy in the new field, singing in that most dearly loved of all oratorios, 'The Messiah' of Händel.

It was immediately after the 'Messiah' performance that she crossed the ocean, her first American concert being sung at Castle Garden, New York City, on September 1, 1850. She remained in America until May 24, 1852, when she made her last appearance in New York. During her stay in the United States, on February 5, 1852, she married, in Boston, the young German pianist, Otto Goldschmidt.

After returning from America, Jenny Lind and her husband lived for three years in Dresden, but Jenny had fallen in love with England — then at the height of its haircloth, Victorian splendor — and in 1856 she returned to its shores, thenceforth to call it home. In her later years she was much more interested in teaching than in singing. From 1876 to 1883, a good share of her energy was invested in leading and training the sopranos of the Bach Choir of which her husband was founder and director, and from 1883 to 1886, she taught singing at the Royal College of Music. Her last public concert was at Malvern Hills, where she lived, on July 23, 1880. It was in this place that the young Ford Madox Ford first saw her one day, and in a sadly faded aspect: 'When I was a boy

19

at Malvern my grandfather went about in a
bath chair because he was suffering from a bad
attack of gout. Sometimes beside his chair another would be pulled along. It contained a
little old lady with a faint and piping voice.
That was Jenny Lind.' She died at Malvern,
after a long and distressing illness, on November
2, 1887.[30]

IV

It is clear enough that any one who was so
prominently before the eyes of her generation
as was Jenny Lind must be from some point of
view an instructive study. To untold thousands
of her contemporaries, she typified the very
highest in both the art and the womanhood of
her day.

Our own first question is, however, a somewhat skeptical one. How much of the Jenny
Lind enthusiasm was genuine, spontaneous, a
direct response to the compelling power of the
artist, and how much of it was deliberately
manufactured and manipulated? At some point
this question enters into the interpretation of
every theatrical celebrity: untheatrical as Jenny
Lind herself was, it can hardly be avoided here.

It must be frankly admitted that Barnum

20

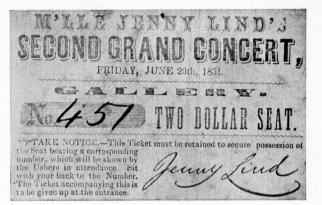

SEAT CHECK FOR A CONCERT

in America used all the devices the showman knows to awaken interest in Jenny Lind and fan it to fever heat. Her talent, her European reputation, her goodness of heart, her sterling character — he made the finest possible use of them all. In England, too, the long dispute over contracts, preceding her début, had, intentionally or not, created a distinctly adventitious interest in her. But after all allowances have been made, the fact remains that this woman must have given her contemporaries something that nobody else gave them in the same degree. The press agent can do a good deal toward stimulating curiosity, but curiosity is not devotion. Even he can hardly take a nobody and make two continents see her as a kind of combination of the Beatrice of the 'Commedia' and all the nine Muses.

In studying Jenny Lind, it is extremely important to establish a point of view. Nothing could be easier than simply to laugh at the whole thing as one more manifestation of the naïve stupidity of our ancestors. And in the long run nothing could be cheaper or more unprofitable. For we are the sons of our ancestors, and children have been known sometimes to take after their parents. I suppose we shall find a good deal of Victorian foolishness before we have done with Jenny Lind. But I hope we shall laugh at such things, when we find them, because they are amusing, and not because they are Victorian. We ought, indeed, to be able to find more humor in those solemn days than their actors found. We are entitled to some compensation for being obliged to live in these days. And if we are able to direct the cool white light of intelligence upon the vagaries of the fathers now and then, it will do them no harm and may do us some good. But the fact that Jenny Lind was brought to America by Barnum would be no excuse for treating her as if she were a side-show in a circus. She was a serious artist, a great artist, and with all her amusing foibles, which will have their place in this portrait, she was an impressive human being as well. It would be a simple thing to create a portrait of her which should reflect the viewpoint of the writer and of the writer's period. Any portrait must inevitably do that. The difficult thing and the thing worth doing is to catch the spirit of her own day, to place her in her proper setting, to set her forth upon her own terms. Only on that basis can any interpretation that is worth anything be constructed.

II
THE ARTIST

To be able to sing, the whole personality must be developed.
So is it with every thing in life if we would reach any sort of *beginning of perfection*. We must look widely around us; no one-sided development. Anyone who wishes to master vocal art, must study many other things. Singing is a peculiar gift more difficult to develop than is believed.

JENNY LIND, 1868

J'en connais même qui chantent mieux; mais aucune ne chante comme elle.

HENRI BLAZE DE BURY

But what did no less astonish me was her Acting, it being as good as her Singing; for she did seem to forget herself in her part, instead of her part in herself; which is the Mistake of most Opera Singers.... But she do throw a Grace and Beauty of her own into the Character and Musique.

'Mr. Pips, his Diary,' *Punch*, 1849

... I cannot say that her voice was so full a one as I expected, or so powerful; her wonderful power over it seemed the great point. She could positively do anything with it. It was absolutely obedient; I never heard anything at all equal to its flexibility; she tossed it about as conjurors do their balls, and seemed to have twenty voices at once. She shook with such perfection that the note seemed self-undulating.... Then she imitated an echo, first a slow, then a quicker one, till the echo of the last note was, as in the case of the real echo, mixed with the succeeding note. Then she had astonishing powers of sustaining long slow notes, which she displayed in the song from Weber.

J. B. MOZLEY

CHAPTER II

The Artist

I

IN considering Jenny Lind as artist, it would be most unwarranted to assume that her popularity was due to her art alone. It was too universal, too far-reaching for that: there are not enough people in the world who are sensitive to purely æsthetic values. 'Other famous singers,' writes George William Curtis, 'charmed that happy time. But Jenny Lind, rivalling their art, went beyond them all in touching the heart with her personality.' [1] And Barnum himself remarked, looking back upon the event from 1890: 'It is a mistake to say the fame of Jenny Lind rests solely upon her ability to sing. She was a woman who would have been adored if she had had the voice of a crow.' [2]

In some respects, of course, this is the finest tribute that could have been paid to her — or to any artist — for the great secret about the artist is that if he is only an artist he is nothing. There are many good singers and good actors, but there are not too many great souls in the

25

world, and when a woman can give her audiences the impression that through her they have caught a glimpse of the beauty of the spirit, who cares whether or not she has presented a masterful characterization? The frequent critical outbursts about personality having run wild in our contemporary theater may safely be set down as so much nonsense: our actors are ten times better than our plays and a hundred times better than our producers. What we need in the theater is not less personality but more — more of the Jenny Lind sort — for the theater lives in a world of personality, and once the direct and personal appeal of the artist to his audience has gone out of it, it must surely die.

But with regard to Miss Lind, the discussion can hardly stop there. One of her Swedish biographers, Norlind, has developed ably and in some detail the thesis that she served her time as the avatar of a romantic ideal, expressing the tendency toward simplification, the union of art and religion so profoundly characteristic of the whole romantic movement, and that in no other period could the gifts that she possessed have awakened quite the response that they did just then. I think there can be little doubt that he is substantially right, but he opens

26

JENNY LIND

up vistas that lie properly beyond the bounds
of my province in this study. Many of Miss
Lind's hearers, in America at least, were not
capable of judging her as a vocalist, and even
had the requisite taste and knowledge been
present, they could hardly have been brought
to bear upon the problem while the audience
was under the spell of the extraordinary emotional intensity that habitually accompanied
her performances. We are told that when she
sang the 'Casta Diva' at Castle Garden, 'the
audience was so completely carried away by
their feelings,' that the last part of the air 'was
drowned in a perfect tempest of acclamation.' [3]
The story seems almost unbelievable, but theatrical manners were notoriously bad in those
days. It must have been a horrible experience
for her, and for any one sensitive to music. And
in Baltimore, when Barnum's daughter, who
was in no way an unusual singer, appeared in a
church choir and was somehow mistaken for
Jenny Lind, quite the same kind of ecstasy is
said to have been observed as manifested itself
habitually in the authentic concerts.[4]

Our difficulty today in really understanding
her vogue is, of course, tremendously increased
by the fact that we have nothing to which we

can actually compare it. It is not that we have
lacked extremely popular singers in our own
land and our own time. The demonstrations
accorded Miss Geraldine Farrar upon her farewell performances at the Metropolitan Opera
House in 1922, for example, and the even more
beautiful reception that awaited her when she
returned to the concert stage five years later,
would seem to afford ample evidence that at
least one singer has appealed very profoundly
to our affections. And there have been others
— Miss Garden, Madame Schumann-Heink,
Mr. McCormack — who, if they have never
achieved quite the adoration that has been bestowed upon Miss Farrar, have nevertheless had
distinguished careers into which the personal
element has entered in an unmistakable way.
In England, moreover, there is Clara Butt, and
to Clara Butt almost regal honors have from
time to time been paid. When she was married
in Bristol in 1900, 'the whole city was turned
upside-down to do her honour; factories, shops,
and offices were given a half-holiday, all the
church-bells set ringing, streets blocked, a
cathedral crammed with duchesses, *prima donnas*,
and what not, special trains to London, a
citizens' presentation, another from the Handel

Festival Choir, and hundreds of presents, including one from the Queen!' 5 Yet I suppose no one would seriously claim that Clara Butt or Geraldine Farrar or Mary Garden has held in our contemporary world of music the position that belonged to Jenny Lind two and a half generations ago.

Indeed, the complex, dismaying conditions of modern life seem, increasingly, to throw their imponderable influence against such eminence. Dame Butt's marriage, for example, is already a generation behind us: one may perhaps be permitted to doubt whether the genuine enthusiasm it awakened could quite be duplicated today. We have become very critical, very sophisticated in our theaters and opera houses: we are not too easily moved. Sometimes we assume that we have no actors who are the equals of those who enthralled our grandfathers, but it is at least a fair possibility that the trouble may lie in the audience rather than across the footlights, that we may have lost, and are losing increasingly, the capacity for rapture that our grandfathers had. It is not without significance that in the United States at least the legitimate theater and the opera seem more and more to be passing into the exclusive possession of the more cultured and more prosperous classes in a few large centers of population. And these are of all Americans the ones who are least susceptible to enthusiasm.

To be sure, we have the motion picture, and the motion picture has done more than it has ever been possible to do before to make dramatic art the common possession of all the people, to create, for the first time, the possibility of an actor's playing to a world-wide audience. Mr. Cyril Maude is celebrated, among other things, for having performed 'Grumpy' in the legitimate theater some 1300 times. But when the talking-picture version of 'Grumpy' was completed recently, with Mr. Maude in it, the 'New York Times' calculated that it would probably be exhibited some 5700 times in the week of its release, and that before being thrown into the discard, it would have had about 150,000 performances in the United States and Canada alone. Is it any wonder that, with the exception of a few outstanding politicians and industrialists, motion-picture actors and actresses are the only persons who are known to everybody in the United States?

There has, indeed, been one career in motion pictures which it seems to me suggestive to study in connection with that of Jenny Lind, and that is the career of Miss Mary Pickford. I speak now not so much of the Mary Pickford of today as of the Mary Pickford of a dozen years ago, the Mary Pickford who is already something of a legendary figure. The motion picture is such an amazing mushroom growth that centuries have been lived through within the life-span of our generation. D'Annunzio's 'Cabiria,' the great Italian spectacle, produced about 1912, has already taken on something of the antique flavor of an eighteenth-century novel, and D. W. Griffith's 'The Birth of a Nation,' first exhibited in 1915, seems a great historic landmark. It may be, therefore, that you who read these lines do not realize quite what Mary Pickford meant to those of us who were born about 1900. We never thought of her as an actress, and if you had asked us if we thought she was an artist, we shouldn't, in those innocent days, have had the faintest idea what you were talking about. She was a presence; she was an ideal; she was an experience. She has been — to a large extent she still is — the only actress of our time who cannot travel from one city to another without stopping the traffic wherever she appears. She was like Jenny Lind

31

always in the virginal something there was about her, in the charities for which she was celebrated, in the fact that, though she was a great charmer, she was entirely lacking in what the distinguished *impresarios* of her profession denominated 'sex-appeal,' and — again like Jenny Lind — she appealed to at least her more devoted followers on the ground of their highest and purest emotions. Vachel Lindsay, writing in 1917, expressed the general attitude toward her in his famous 'New Republic' article called 'Queen of My People.'⁶ 'To reject this girl in haste,' he declared, 'is high treason to the national heart.' And in Brooklyn, New York, a lonely little red-haired girl, all unaware of the spectacular career she herself was to experience on the screens of the world, was, even then, learning to use the motion picture as a means of escape from her own drab surroundings, and characteristically choosing Mary Pickford as the embodiment of her ideal. 'Maybe there really were people like that in the world.' That experience of Miss Clara Bow was typical of an entire generation. Indeed the whole Mary Pickford vogue was a sociological phenomenon of the highest importance, and it has never been studied with half the seriousness it deserves. In its own way, it throws quite as much light on the national psychology in the years leading up to and during the World War as does our devotion to Theodore Roosevelt or the amazing career of William Jennings Bryan.

It can never happen again. Never again, not even in the movies. It is not that we no longer have anybody who is worthy to inspire it. No one who has felt the wistful charm of Miss Janet Gaynor, no one who has been touched by the humane and sensitive loveliness of Miss Joan Bennett, can suppose for a moment that the newest generation in the theater is in any sense destitute of a precious radiance of personality. 'In anything fit to be called by the name of reading,' remarked Robert Louis Stevenson, in 'A Gossip on Romance,' 'the process itself should be absorbing and voluptuous; we should gloat over a book, be rapt clean out of ourselves, and rise from the perusal, our mind filled with the busiest, kaleidoscopic dance of images, incapable of sleep or of continuous thought.' If he was right, then the habit of 'critical reading' that we are doing our best to teach to young people in all our schools and universities is certainly going to lead to a prodigious destruction of literary appreciation! Stevenson's ideal

33

lingered on in the theater for some time after it had perished in the library: in this instance, at least, mob psychology came to the aid of art. And even after Shaw and Ibsen had taught the intelligentsia that the theater is a laboratory and a dissecting-room, and that nobody save an abandoned and empty-headed profligate would dream of going there for pleasure, zest and passion lived on for a generation longer in the motion-picture theaters of the world, with their immensely more popular audience and their superb disregard of all 'artistic' toff. It is not by any means an accident that some of the greatest successes of the motion picture have been based on material immensely popular in the legitimate theater twenty to thirty years ago. Now all that is seen in the act of passing. The intelligentsia have taken up the motion picture and are already beginning to ruin it as they long ago ruined everything else. Even at Hogan's Corners they are talking about 'technique' and 'criticism' and 'décor,' condemning players because they are 'mike-conscious,' ruthlessly dismissing that which is not 'authentic cinema,' and in general employing 'such abominable words as no Christian ear can endure to hear.' How long do you suppose the spirit of adoration

34

can survive in such an atmosphere? It is no accident that the most popular screen actress of these latter days — the girl who above all others has expressed the laughter and the heartbreak of our time, should, all too often, have been greeted with cruel gossip and slander, rather than with the appreciation that was her due.

Even in the Golden Age, however, the movies cannot carry us all the way in understanding Jenny Lind. For Miss Pickford's popularity, in the years before the War, was a thing wholly of the people: her following was made up largely of young persons, high-school girls and boys like myself, and, in general, of those inexperienced in the arts. Her sociological importance, as I have already suggested, her influence on the tastes and ideals of the generation recently come into maturity, has been, for that very reason, enormous: as an artist, she never carried outside the world of motion pictures themselves. In speaking thus, I need hardly add, I imply no disparagement to Miss Pickford. Nor do I when I discuss the Pickford cult as largely an historical phenomenon. So gifted an artist may safely be trusted to hold her own amid any conditions. If the public, these latter days, is in-

35

clined somewhat to run after strange gods, it is
not so much that she has changed as it is they
have changed themselves. And, I confess, I can
hardly persuade myself that the change is for
the better. The significant difference between
Pickford and Lind, however, is this, that the
latter's was never, in any sense, an untrained
audience. She had the masses, not so completely
as Miss Pickford had them, because she lacked
the enormous advantage which fell to the
motion-picture actress in the mechanical re-
production of her art, but still far more profoundly than any other singer had ever had
them. And then, besides, she appealed greatly
to an overwhelming proportion of the most
prominent men and women, the most brilliant
artists of her day. It is time to examine a few of
these testimonies.

II

'As a singer,' wrote Washington Irving, 'she
appears to me of the very first order; as a speci-
men of womankind, a little more. She is enough
of herself to counterbalance of all the evil that
the world is threatened with by the great con-
vention of women.' [7] Longfellow declared:
'She is very feminine and lovely. Her power is

JENNY LIND AS THE DAUGHTER OF THE REGIMENT

in her presence, which is magnetic, and takes her audience captive before she opens her lips. She sings like the morning star; clear, liquid, heavenly sounds.' [8] Queen Victoria expressed her views in a letter to the King of the Belgians: 'Poor Grisi is quite going off, and after the pure angelic voice and extremely quiet, perfect acting of J. Lind, she seems quite passée.' [9] About the same time, Macready recorded in his Diary: 'Saw *La Figlia del Reggimento* and Jenny Lind — the most charming singer and actress I have ever in my life seen. Her energy, vivacity, archness, humour, passion, and pathos are equally true.' [10] The great musicians of the Continent had capitulated almost to a man. Chopin declared: 'The Swedish lady is an original from top to toe. Her presence seems pervaded by the magic atmosphere of the North. Her singing is invariably pure and true, but what I admired most is her *piano* which is indescribably fascinating.' [11] Best of all is the tribute of Mendelssohn: 'She is as great an artist as ever lived; and the greatest I have known.' [12]

Of course there are dissenting voices, since the world agrees only with regard to absolute mediocrity. But it is perfectly evident — here as clearly as in the very different case of Sarah

37

Bernhardt — that what we have, in every such instance, is definitely dissent, that is, a departure from the usual standard or norm of judgment. Hawthorne heard her, and 'on the whole, was not very much interested in her.' [13] You would hardly have expected him to be. Carlyle's reaction was very Carlylean: 'a very true, clear, genuine little creature, with a voice of extraordinary *extent* and *little* richness of tone; who sang, acted, etc., with consummate fidelity, but had unfortunately nothing but mere *non*sense to sing or act....' [14] Thackeray found her 'atrociously stupid. I was thinking of something else the whole time she was jugulating away, and O! I was so glad to get to the end and have a cigar....' [15] Gentlemen who are longing for a cigar have never been particularly good judges of musical affairs.

Whitman's objection, and Richard Wagner's, are entitled to more respect. The American wrote in the 'New York Evening Post': 'The Swedish Swan, with all her blandishments, never touched my heart in the least. I wondered at so much vocal dexterity; and indeed they were all very pretty, those leaps and double somersets. But even in the grandest religious airs, genuine masterpieces as they are, of the

German composers, executed by this strangely
overpraised woman in perfect scientific style,
let critics say what they like, it was a failure; for
there was a vacuum in the head of the performance. Beauty pervaded it no doubt, and
that of a high order. It was the beauty of Adam
before God breathed into his nostrils.' [16] This,
as I say, deserves respectful consideration, yet
I hardly think Whitman is a safe guide. He
dissented in precisely the same way with regard
to Edwin Booth.[17] Wagner heard Jenny Lind
in 'Don Giovanni' in 1845 and wrote to his
wife: 'She has a curious pensive individuality,
which interests one much in itself, but cannot
rise to a great dramatic portrayal.' [18] On a
different level altogether is the dissent of Mrs.
Jameson, which seems to have a powerful
amount of pig-headed determination about it:
'I don't and won't admire Jenny Lind whose
success has been of a kind to make all such
triumphs ridiculous. She is an accomplished
singer and *second-rate* actress; we have had so
many better!' [19]

It is a striking fact, however, that on the rare
occasions when Jenny Lind faced a cold and a
hostile audience, she conquered it completely.
Such was the case at Philadelphia, where the

39

public had determined in advance that it was not going to allow itself to be carried away and stampeded into extravagant praise as had been the case in Boston and in New York, but where, once she had begun to sing, her reception was as enthusiastic as any that had been vouchsafed her; and it was notably the case in Havana, where the opposition to Barnum had gone to the length of determined, ill-mannered hostility, involving cat-calls and all the other resources of theatrical bad manners, but here again her success was sensational, and the nonplussed Cubans found themselves begging humbly and vainly for more concerts.

There are critics and writers, however, who, while warmly appreciating Jenny Lind, and paying tribute to the splendor of her gifts as having greatly enriched their artistic experience, yet insist that she had very pronounced limitations. Such, for example, is the position of the famous British critic, Henry F. Chorley: 'In short, Mdlle. Lind's opera repertory was limited, — one which must have exposed her on every side to comparisons should she have remained on the stage till enthusiasm cooled, as it must inevitably have done. If she became aware of this, and if such conviction had its part

40

in her determination to give up the theatre for the concert room, the conviction was a wise one.' Even in 'La Figlia del Reggimento,' Chorley considered her inferior to Sontag, and he calls her Susanna, in 'Le Nozze di Figaro,' 'stiff, heavy, and conscientious.' [20] Chorley, to be sure, was not Jenny's most sympathetic reviewer, but he was an able critic and he cannot be too lightly dismissed, especially since he fully appreciated her Julia, in 'La Vestale' — the rôle which she herself considered her finest piece of work [21] — 'a real, pathetic, admirable piece of acting — by much her best tragic character.' [22] Similarly, Sir Julius Benedict, who played accompaniments for her in America, names five rôles: Alice, in 'Roberto il Diavolo,' Amina, in 'La Sonnambula,' Marie, in 'La Figlia del Reggimento,' Lucia, in 'Lucia di Lammermoor,' and Elvira, in 'L'Elisir d'Amore' — as the only ones in which 'she held an undisputed sway over her audiences.' [23] Even the entirely sympathetic Longfellow found it advisable to discriminate: 'Jenny Lind has a Northern soul and sings Northern music better than Southern.' [24]

Like others who think it necessary to express their own personalities in the rôles that they

enact, Jenny Lind sometimes failed in por-
traying a character with which she herself was
not in perfect sympathy. This seems to have
been the case in an 1846 performance of 'Les
Huguenots.' 'However many various characters may be in sympathy with her individuality,
she seemed unwilling to identify herself with
that of the Court-lady.' Not until the third act,
'when she emerges from the natural forms of
life to plunge into the depths of the inner
world with all its profoundest impressions' did
she begin to give a satisfactory performance.[25]
Sometimes, as in the case of Norma, she re-
charactered a rôle in order to bring it more into
harmony with her own tastes and point of view.
Macready found her Norma 'very womanly,
loving, passionate, and grand,' but doubted
'whether it will be a *popular* performance — it
wants more vulgar effect to be so....'[26] Most
observers agreed with Macready that Miss
Lind's Norma was 'womanly' and 'loving,' but
the heroic elements of passion and grandeur
were not, in England at least, felt to be very
conspicuous. Parker Willis, who adored her,
found even the 'Casta Diva,' which she sang so
often in her concerts, deficient in this regard.
'On Jenny's lips,' wrote Willis, 'the devout

purity and imploring worship and contrition, proper to the stanzas in which the Deity is addressed, are continued throughout; and the Roman, who has both desecrated and been faithless to her, is besought to return and sin again, with accents of sublimely unconscious innocence.' [27]

III

It is fortunately not necessary for me to undertake any very detailed technical description of Jenny Lind's voice.[28] She possessed the extraordinary range of two octaves and three quarters, from B below the staff to G in the fourth line above it. Her high F sharps were of unusual beauty, and it was with the idea of displaying them to best advantage that Mendelssohn composed his 'Hear ye, Israel.' The upper A appeared prominently in a syncopated passage in a 'Casta Diva' cadence, as well as in one of her Swedish songs. She always improvised her *cadenzas*, which most hearers found beautiful and in excellent taste, an exception being Sir Julius Benedict, who writes, somewhat strangely, that in 'La Sonnambula,' 'her elaborate Scandinavian *cadenzas* jarred sometimes with the ideas, so true and passionate, of

43

the Italian composer.' [29] I confess I have not
yet discovered anything particularly sacrosanct
in 'La Sonnambula,' nor am I prepared to say
just what is particularly Scandinavian about a
cadenza. She was famous for her 'shake' or
'trill,' her *messa di voce*, and, above all, for her
pianissimo singing, which, 'though falling on the
ear like a whisper, reached the farthest corner
of theatre or concert room.' [30]

What we are much more interested in, however, is what might be called the individuality
of her singing, its connotations, as it were, the
ideas it awakened and the emotions to which it
appealed. And of all this it is obvious that I,
who never heard Jenny Lind, can give only a
very unsatisfactory report to a generation none
of whose members have ever heard her either.
You may say that Madame Galli-Curci sings —
or used to sing — like a flute, that there was a
'cello-like quality in the voice of Madame Alma
Gluck, and those who have heard these singers
will understand what you mean and agree with
you, but the comparisons could convey very
little meaning to those who have no memories.
The musical critic, indeed, is always seeking to
do the impossible. Straight literary criticism is
comparatively easy, for here the medium in

44

JENNY LIND AS AMINA IN 'LA SONNAMBULA'

which the experience exists, and the medium in which it must be described, are identical — words. But musical criticism is cruelly, infernally difficult always — in fact, it can hardly be said to exist. And the reason is perfectly simple: an æsthetic experience conveyed through one channel of apprehension can hardly be described in terms of another. Newspaper critics in general recognize this situation quite frankly, giving, when they are bad, mere 'reports' of concerts and operas, and when they are good, presenting interesting little essays into which the discussion of technical matters does not enter very deeply. Many of our most successful reviewers, indeed, never attempt anything save to describe in words the emotion with which a musical performance has left them.[31]

We often hear it said that the autobiographies of musicians are devoid of musical interest, being devoted instead to mere gossipy sketches of social contacts. Often the objector falls into the error of censuring the musician, and deciding that so far as music is concerned, he must be a very shallow fellow after all. The absurdity of the judgment is patent: the trouble is with music, not with the musician. He is generally an untrained writer: how can you expect him

45

to succeed where those who have devoted their lives to the business of criticism have failed? Indeed, the ideal criticism of a piece of music is never in words: it is in another piece of music — serious or the reverse — in which an impression of the first is embodied. The outrageous sentimentality of Chopin — and of many another romantic composer — has been 'criticized' often enough in a popular love song. To a certain extent, to be sure, the same difficulties are encountered by the critic who devotes his attention to painting and sculpture. They are more easily surmountable in this field, however — witness the respectable bulk of art criticism in our libraries — through various devices which it would carry me too far afield to discuss here. For one thing, the art critic, realizing that language, which exists in a world of time, not space, is supremely fitted for narration, not for description, frequently very wisely casts his descriptions into the narrative form. The trick is a very old one, and its use is not confined to critics: Homer employed it in one of the most famous pieces of descriptive writing in the world: the picture of the shield of Achilles in the 'Iliad.' [32]

But to come back to the quality of Miss Lind's

singing. 'As I remember her voice,' wrote Richard Hoffman, who assisted in the American concerts, 'it was not so brilliant as it was deliciously rounded, and of an exquisite musical timbre. It possessed great volume, and what seemed an inexhaustible reserve force.' [33] Another writes: 'Its timbre was like a clarinet, penetrating and tearful and sweet, and it flowed out with great volume and power.' And again: 'She possessed two qualities of voice — one sombre, the other of a clear, sunny ring, brilliant and sparkling. She carried her middle voice in one quality up to high B flat without a break, and sang there in the same rich tone as in her middle octaves.' [34] And even Garcia said that when she sang 'Come unto me,' the first notes 'were so full, pure, and perfect in intonation that the refrain which preceded them sounded out of tune.' [35]

Others report more directly their own emotional reaction. So richly gifted, so highly sensitive a man as John Addington Symonds could write: 'At the first tones of her voice, I quivered all over. It is not her wonderful execution, her pathos, varying expression, subtle flexibility, that surprised me, but the pure timbre which so vibrated and thrilled my very soul that tears

47

came into my eyes.' [36]   And Henry Cabot
Lodge always remembered her as he heard her
in his youth, on a European holiday: 'She was a
plain woman, very simply dressed, and looked
elderly to my youthful eyes. She sang, among
other things, one or two English songs, which I
particularly remember, and her voice seemed
to me the most wonderful I had ever listened to.
It had a quality of beauty which dwells with me
still and which I have never heard surpassed.' [37]

It is evident that Nature was kind to Jenny
Lind in giving her what is fundamental to
achievement in music — I mean ear and a certain natural musicianship. I know there have
been great singers, many of them, who were not
naturally musical. But such a singer labors always under a terrific handicap. Jenny Lind
was musical. When she was only three years
old, she reproduced on the piano a fanfare she
had heard from the military bugles in the street.
Nor did she ever forget the passage: years later,
she wrote it down for her daughter.[38] And in
her maturity the Schumanns were literally
dumbfounded when she sang two of Robert's
greatest songs, 'Marienwürmchen' and 'Früh-
lingsglaube,' at sight, and sang them magnificently.[39]

48

As late as 1861, so good a musician as Moscheles pronounces her voice 'as fine as ever.' [40] But she was not the kind of singer whose appeal depends on her technical dexterity, on the sensuous beauty of her tones alone. Lady Frederick Cavendish heard her in 1863. 'I suppose her high notes are a little gone,' she writes, 'but the matchless expression and *heart-feeling* can never go out of her voice, and there is a ringing purity of tone unlike anything else.' [41] And when Lady Westmorland heard gossip to the effect that Jenny had lost her voice, she said: 'Never mind; if she has still got her soul, she is better worth hearing than all the other singers of the world.' [42] How many artists are there in any generation about whom any human being feels like that?

IV

But Nature did not give her everything, nor did Nature do her work for her. The continual comparison to the nightingale, much as she relished it, did not quite cover the case. When we say that a woman sings like a bird, we are generally intending a compliment, but we can hardly be said to pay any very warm tribute to the directing intelligence behind the mere

49

sensuous beauty. The technical chapter in the authorized biography, as well as the recently published letter written in 1868 to Professor Bystrom,[43] makes it abundantly clear that Jenny Lind analyzed her voice down to its minutest detail, knew its strength and its weakness, and built it up consciously to what it ultimately became. She had begun singing in Sweden without adequate training, sang, indeed, until she almost wore out her voice. When she arrived in Paris, Garcia refused even to consider her as a pupil until her vocal organs had had six weeks of absolute rest, yet in later years he was to tell his biographer that 'he had never heard her sing even a hair's-breadth out of tune, so perfect was her natural ear.' Nor did she ever repeat an error, once it had been pointed out to her. 'Jenny Lind would have cut her throat sooner than have given me reason to say, "We corrected that mistake last time."'[44] Nature had not given her an especially large lung capacity: such triumphs as she won here were due, not to native endowment, but to a skillful management of her breath control, so that it is said she learned to breathe in such a way that the spectator could not detect the moment at which the breath was renewed.

'For twenty-five years,' she wrote in the letter to Bystrom, 'have I steadily worked on the chromatic scale and only five or six years ago did it come perfectly — when I no longer needed it.' Clara Louise Kellogg reports Benedict telling her that Jenny Lind had a 'hole' in her voice, and that he had always to play her accompaniments in such a way as to cover it up.[45] But Benedict seems sometimes to have had rather odd ideas. When Jenny Lind was in her prime, a certain veiled quality in the middle register is the only technical deficiency to which one finds others referring.

Certainly there can be no question concerning her devotion to her task, her willingness to work. 'If I had nothing but music in the world,' she says, 'it would be enough.' [46] No detail was too insignificant to demand and to receive hours of study if necessary. Thus she once practiced on the word *zersplittre* on a high B flat in the opening recitative of 'Norma' for several hours at a stretch. And to the end of her career, she always rehearsed during the day the opera that she was to sing at night.[47] When she began her work with Garcia, she was already a famous singer in her own country, but they went back to fundamentals, quite as remorselessly as if she had never sung a note. 'I have to begin again, from the beginning; to sing scales, up and down, slowly, and with great care; then, to practice the shake — awfully slowly; and to try to get rid of the hoarseness, if possible. Moreover, he is very particular about the breathing. I trust I have made a happy choice. Anyhow, he is the best master; and expensive enough — twenty francs for an hour. But, what does that signify, if only he can teach me to sing?' [48] Benedict says she invariably did her best: at Natchez and at Memphis, where they had small audiences, largely colored, she was every bit as conscientious as she had been in Boston and New York. When he mentioned the circumstance to her, she replied: 'I value my art much too highly to degrade it even occasionally by any wilful disregard of what I consider due to it.' [49] Chorley speaks of this same conscientiousness, though he is by no means sure that it always improved her performances. 'Of all the singers whom I have ever heard Mdlle. Lind was perhaps the most assiduous. Her resolution to offer the very best of her best to her public seemed part and parcel of her nature and of her conscience. Not a note was neglected by her, not a phrase slurred over.

52

Unlike many of the Italians, who spare themselves in uninteresting passages of any given
opera to shine out in some favorite piece of display, she went through her entire part with a
zeal which it was impossible not to admire, and
which could not be too generally adopted as a
principle by every one, great and small, who
presents himself to an audience. But perhaps
owing to this remarkable strenuousness, many
of her effects on the stage appeared overcal-
culated. Everything was brought out into an
equally high relief.' 50

Considering the brevity of Jenny Lind's
operatic career, her repertory of thirty operas
seems unusually large. The opera-goer of today
looks at it with a somewhat unfamiliar eye, yet
'Lucia di Lammermoor,' 'Il Flauto Magico,'
'Don Giovanni,' 'Le Nozze di Figaro,' 'L'Elisir
d'Amore,' 'Les Huguenots,' and 'I Puritani'
still find employment among us, and most of us
have some recollection — if only thanks to the
Victrola — of 'La Sonnambula,' 'Roberto il
Diavolo,' 'La Figlia del Reggimento,' 'Der
Freischütz,' 'Euryanthe,' 'Semiramide,' and
'La Vestale.' The rest of the list is dead enough,
I am afraid, and probably deserves to be,
though it is difficult to dogmatize concerning

53

unfamiliar material. In opera, Jenny Lind was
not herself in control of the pieces in which she
appeared, nor would it be fair to infer her own
tastes from them. In 1846, she permitted herself to appear in Vienna in 'Die Ghibellinen
in Pisa,' a bastard version of 'Les Huguenots.'
But the one occasion in her career when her
common-sense seems completely to have de-
serted her was when, having determined to
leave opera, she consented to give, at Her
Majesty's in London, a series of 'Grand Classical Performances' which were to be nothing
else than that desperate form of entertainment,
opera 'in concert form.' The opening bill was
'Il Flauto Magico,' and with it Jenny met her
first and only popular failure. In fairness to
her, it should be noted that she was at the time
strongly under the influence of one Captain
Claudius Harris, of whom we shall have much
hereafter, and also that so good a musician as
Arthur Coleridge rated the performance a high
musical achievement.[51] Miss Lind herself recognized her error almost immediately and
agreed to offer a series of farewell performances
on the operatic stage.

Her own musical preferences may be more
fairly inferred from her concert programmes.

54

In early life, at least, her natural tastes in music were not austere. When she was a child, military music had always delighted her, and her biographers tell us that even in later years the sight of a regiment of soldiers never failed to thrill her. Sir Charles Hallé's opinion is very suggestive at this point: 'Whether her judgment in music kept pace with her marvellous genius as a singer I have not been able to decide, for I have seen her cry when hearing a beautiful masterpiece well sung by a good chorus, and seen her cry also when some very commonplace ditty was given by the same chorus.' [52] And Appy speaks of her 'childlike simplicity of character' as being best expressed in her ballad singing. [53]

Certainly it was the ballads which, in America at least, made the widest appeal to the great bulk of her audiences. And to us who come fresh from one of Miss Geraldine Farrar's incomparable Lieder programmes or from one of Mr. Edward Johnson's balanced, scholarly recitals, some of Miss Lind's concerts do seem a little thin, especially in the first part of her career, before she was relying, to any large extent, upon the Lieder. Take, for example, the opening performance in New York. The

Casta Diva' to begin with, and that was splendid, even audacious enough. What soprano today would dare to open a programme with the 'Casta Diva'? But what came afterwards? A duet with Belletti from 'Il Turco in Italia,' a Swedish song, and a miserable 'Welcome to America,' the music of which had been hastily improvised by Sir Julius Benedict. And that was all. The 'Welcome to America' was Barnum's fault. She sang it under protest: she could not have refused without seriously wounding him and jeopardizing the success of her tour at the outset.⁵⁴ But at her last concert in New York she did something quite as bad on her own responsibility when she sang a 'Farewell to America,' composed for the occasion by C. P. Cranch. Once she even suffered Barnum to persuade her to offer 'Hail, Columbia,' and we are told that her 'interpretation' was not good, so that she did not even have the vulgar reward of pleasing the audience in return for this outrage.⁵⁵

Taken in the large, however, the range of Miss Lind's musical interests looms up much more impressively than these scattered instances, taken by themselves, might indicate. She began with music of the Meyerbeer type,

JENNY LIND
GIOVANNI BELLETTI
AND JULES BENEDICT

but as time went on she won distinction as an interpreter of Mozart ('the Divine Mozart,' she called him), of Mendelssohn, of Händel and Haydn, of Schubert, of Schumann, and finally of Bach. In 1876, when, under the direction of her husband, Bach's 'Mass in B Minor' was first given in England in its complete form, she personally led and trained the sopranos in the choir, which certainly does not sound like the prima donna who is interested only in herself or who is indifferent to high musical values either. From Meyerbeer to Bach is quite a jump, and there is no doubt that Jenny Lind did grow and develop along this line. Being a very positive person, she had, however, always her blind spots and her prejudices. One of them was Brahms and another was Wagner, whose music she considered injurious to the voice. The 'new music' of her later years did not please her in any way, and like many elderly singers, she persuaded herself that musical art was decadent, simply because the style had changed. 'Where are there now any song-composers,' she asked in 1881, 'since Bellini, Rossini, Donizetti, Lindblad, and Josephson are gone? At that time there was song-music — now there is music which is *supposed* to be song; it is purely harmonic difficulties which disregard the simple and the beautiful.' [56]   Her daughter, Mrs. Maude, sums up the whole thing succinctly when she writes: 'Mlle. Lind's sympathies were entirely with the Italian school of singing as against the German....' [57]

V

But the operatic artist must be much more than a singer. Jenny Lind never fell into the error of assuming that if only a woman possessed a beautiful voice, that all was that she needed to interest her audience. 'Why have a glorious voice,' asks Miss Farrar, 'and when you come on the stage look like something which has been delivered by auto truck?' [58]   We generally date the clear recognition of the importance of acting on the operatic stage from the influential example of Madame Emma Calvé, and in these latter days there have been careers, notably that of Miss Mary Garden, in which the dramatic interests have far outweighed any purely musical considerations. But Jenny Lind's admirers seem to have been enthralled by her acting almost as much as by her voice: indeed, she appeared as a child actress in melodramas long before she ever sang a note on the stage, and until she went to Paris her musicianship was so seriously defective that it would seem as if her early Swedish successes, even after she was classified as a singer, must have been due very largely to her dramatic gifts. That she was capable, even in concert, of a large amount of dramatic versatility appears in Symonds's description of the variety of expression with which she invested her singing of an air from Händel's 'Susannah.' It also suggests that she may have been guilty of over-emphasis. '"Deprived of sun" was barren and triste, with a mournful pleading in the voice, and "cheering air" produced a smile as though to draw a picture of what the poor plant might have enjoyed. Then on the word "wither" her whole frame languished, and the sounds came dying out. "Shall human mind demand less pain?" she gave with fire and indignation.' [59] She had been carefully trained in elocution and dancing, as well as in singing, and she was always extremely impatient of singers who moved awkwardly, who did not articulate clearly, and whose appearance while singing was not pleasant. Her own diction was quite universally praised, and she is said to have articulated with unusual clarity, even when she was singing in

59

a language comparatively unfamiliar to her. Berlioz and Chorley are agreed that as Lucia she was the only singer who prepared the mind of the audience for the climactic scenes of Lucia's madness.[60]

But she was not a good showman. She disliked the artificial aids to effect which the actress habitually employs; sometimes refused, as Duse did, to use even rouge on the stage. In her concerts she invariably wore a simple white dress, and her general aspect suggested simplicity and purity, never the complicated, highly emotionalized set of reactions that we habitually associate with the prima donna. It may be urged, with some measure of acuteness, that all this was, for her, precisely the highest and subtlest kind of showmanship, but while it undoubtedly worked out as such showmanship might, there is not a shred of evidence to indicate that she ever planned it in that way. Only, she considered always the total effect of her personality, not merely the narrower appeal of her voice.

Most observers are agreed that Jenny Lind on the stage was a model of grace and charm. 'I see Jenny Lind gliding down the stage with consummate grace' — writes George P. Upton

— 'she never seemed to walk....' [61] And Richard Hoffman says: 'She had a most attractive personality, and nothing could have been more naïve and charming than her manner on the stage. She would trip on and off, as if in an ecstasy of delight at the opportunity of singing, bowing and smiling to her audience, and giving every one present a flattering sense of contributing in a measure toward the success of the evening.' [62] But there is a minority opinion here which is well represented by Thomas Wentworth Higginson, who describes her, in a letter to his mother, as looking over her audience 'in a half-smiling, thoughtful sort of way, swaying herself a little to and fro, not graceful, but sweet and gentle, tall, slender, with a very unbecoming white dress, and white roses in her hair — a face like all the pictures.' [63] And Appy found her positively awkward on the concert platform and was unable to understand how she could have been considered a great actress in Europe. In later years he remembered her as dancing out onto the stage, and suggests that possibly the reason may have been that she was slightly lame! [64]

Jenny Lind's passionate Puritanism naturally took often the form of a certain honesty. One

notes with a little surprise that she seems to have
acquiesced without protest in several of Barnum's harmless little frauds, as when in order
to spare her the fatigue of battling her way
through the crowds, he passed off his daughter
for her in New Orleans, and again in Philadelphia, when he dressed up another member
of the party in her clothes and exhibited her
as Jenny Lind to an adoring populace from a
balcony.[65] Much more characteristic of her was
what happened at the first concert on her English provincial tour, where the managers had
instructed the assisting artists, who were con-
cealed from the audience, to applaud vigorously
as she finished her number. She was very angry
at the deception, and it was not perpetrated
again.[66]

On the stage she seems to have been even
more honest than she was in life. In 'La Sonnambula' she never permitted a substitute to
cross the bridge for her in the sleep-walking
scene, as was then the custom, but insisted upon
doing it herself, even though the strain un-
nerved her and sometimes interfered with her
singing in the scene immediately following. 'I
should have been ashamed to stand before the
audience,' she said, 'pretending that I had

crossed the bridge, if I had not really done it.' [67]
Here she reminds one of Miss Farrar's refusal to
permit the use of an 'extra' to take, in her be-
half, the physical risks that were demanded in
the production of her motion pictures. 'I would
no more think of having some one substitute for
my "physically violent" scenes in the movies
than I would think of letting another sing my
top notes at the opera.' [68] And here, it seems to
some of us, both ladies have somewhat confused
art with life. The theater is a world of illusion
in any event: it depends upon illusion for its
very existence. Why worry about minor' pre-
tenses like crossing a bridge when your whole
success depends upon your ability to 'pretend'
that you are another person and to express
emotions that you do not really feel at all? But
doubtless it often seems to the sincere actor that
he does feel them. 'I scarcely ever think of the
effect I am producing,' said Jenny Lind, 'and if
the thought does sometimes come across me, it
spoils my acting. It seems to me, when I act,
that I feel fully all the emotions of the character
I represent. I fancy myself — in fact, believe
myself — to be in her situation; and never
think of the audience.' More concretely, when
she was asked about a certain effect in 'Roberto

il Diavolo,' she exclaimed passionately, 'How could I tell how I sang it? I stood at the man's right hand, and the Fiend at his left, and all I could think of was, how to save him.' [69]

It is clear, too, that in her operatic career, Miss Lind never followed tradition blindly, never shrank from introducing a new interpretation of even a well-established rôle when it seemed to her that such departures were in the interest of art and of truth. Her Norma, success or failure as the case may be, was a radically different interpretation from that with which the public was familiar, and the same was true of her Euryanthe. When preparing to appear at Berlin, as Julia in 'La Vestale,' she insisted on many changes in the libretto. And it is said that she was the first to sing the 'Casta Diva' in the key of F, with which it has since been generally identified, rather than in the key of G, in which it was composed.

As to the artistic value of her departures, it was natural that there should have been differences of opinion. In England, Chorley wrote of her that she 'seemed resolved to dominate beyond any artist whom I have ever seen.' [70] Benedict lends color to this view also when he tells us that at the close of 'La Sonnambula,'

JENNY LIND AS ALICE IN 'ROBERTO IL DIAVOLO'

she 'destroyed the effect by doubling the part
of the tenor in order to introduce a few high
notes.' [71]   And Sims Reeves's account of one
horrible feature in her management of 'Lucia di
Lammermoor' is so specific that one can hardly
disbelieve in its substantial accuracy: 'At the
end of the magnificent *finale* to the second act...
Lucia appeals to the indignant Edgardo, who
throws her back into her brother's arms; upon
which the curtain falls. Jenny Lind, however,
as if to concentrate all attention on herself,
rushed to the front of the stage, indicated by her
gestures and general demeanour that she was
losing her reason, and remained, as if demented,
before the footlights, while the curtain fell behind her.' [72]

The judgment of the Continental critics, on
the other hand, does not at all sustain these
views. To be sure, Liszt once refused to conduct a festival at which she was to sing, basing
his objection on the ground that wherever she
appeared, she inevitably absorbed all the attention of the audience.[73] But she and Liszt
seem to have hated each other on general
principles — it may be that the composer's Don
Juan-like tendencies did not help to endear him
to the puritanical Lind — and in any case his

65

objection seems to constitute a rather amusing confession that she was a greater, or at least a more interesting, artist than himself. But, as I say, this is quite exceptional on the Continent. Indeed, the difference seems so striking that one wonders whether in some of her departures Jenny may not have been misjudged in England, may not have been following the Continental tradition rather than indulging in any self-glorification on her own account. In any case, it was the Continentals who felt that she always envisaged her rôle as an entity, a coherent unit, that she never played for points, choosing rather to adjust herself to the interpretation of the opera as a whole and reserving her own striking dramatic effects for a few great situations. In 1844, sending tickets for a performance of 'Armida' to her friend and guardian, Judge Munthe, she wrote: 'Both the music and the piece, are so grand, that my smallness will be shown out, thereby, in its true light. But I am so thrilled by the sublime spirit of the music that I am only too ready to risk my own personality.' [74] I am not greatly impressed by this. Young ladies describing their musical aspirations to their guardians have sometimes been known to speak more modestly than truthfully. But there is some rather cogent testimony to her sincerity in what she *did* when she first appeared as Donna Anna in 'Don Giovanni.' Since the death of Mozart, it had been customary to end this opera with the descent of the hero to hell. Jenny Lind restored the *recitativo secco* which had been expunged in favor of spoken dialogue, and restored also the last three movements of the finale. This necessitated her appearance and that of the other principals in a long and elaborate concerted piece after their solos had been completed — surely an arrangement well calculated to test the loyalty of any singer to any master! [75]

Yet, for all her faithfulness to the composer and all her conscientiousness in attempting to set forth his exact shade of meaning, she never made the mistake of thinking of the interpreter as a mere automaton or in any way minimized his importance. She insisted, as truly vital spirits in the theater are always inclined to insist, on the privilege of coloring her rôle with her own life-experience, of heating it in the fires of her own spirit, and giving it forth marked with a distinctive something that was Jenny Lind and nobody else on earth. In the hands of an incompetent, a foolish, or a self-seeking art-

ist, this method has before now led to some
dreadful results, yet without it in some form
great acting cannot exist. The vulgar theory
that the actor nightly reduces himself to putty
and then proceeds to construct a fresh character
from its foundations — and that a character
into which his own personality does not enter
at all — never appealed to Jenny Lind. She
could never have subscribed to the curious
doctrine of Coquelin, that the actor personally
should feel nothing, and that in so far as he
himself shares the emotions that he desires to
awaken in his audience, the artistic integrity
of his work is marred.[76] If there is any contemporary actor whose example has tended to
show that a flawless technique, cultivated and
developed with superb intelligence and with
untiring zeal, can almost atone in acting for the
lack of a passionate temperament and at times
even become an acceptable substitute for what
our grandfathers called the divine fire, George
Arliss is that man. Yet even George Arliss,
commenting on Coquelin's *credo*, in his introduction to the Columbia University edition of
Fanny Kemble's 'On the Stage,' remarks that
the great Frenchman being what he was, we can
hardly pretend that in his case the theory did

68

not work, yet at the same time indicates very frankly his own dissent. Coquelin was a great actor, no doubt, but such a cool, detached kind of art could never have appealed to Jenny Lind. Possibly she might even have taken it as a fresh piece of evidence of the coldness and degeneracy of the French temper, which she so passionately loathed in any case! Her own ideal was sharply opposed. 'A light within,' 'a power from above,' was for her an absolute necessity; 'for all music, whether it is playing or singing, which does not come from within and go out can never be anything worth listening to. One must oneself feel and oneself experience what one is singing or there is nothing to share with those who listen.' [77] And she told A. P. Stanley that 'she could not leave her own character altogether behind, when she came on the stage; that, to destroy her individuality would destroy all that was good in her; and, that she made it a principle, never to represent such passions as would awaken bad feelings.... But, on the other hand, whatever conception she did form of the character she acted, she threw herself into it entirely. If, as once or twice happened, she was unable to do this, she felt she was acting, and telling lies, and then *entirely failed.*' [78] It would

69

be impossible that *impersonation* and *interpretation* could be placed in sharper contrast to each other. 'To destroy her individuality would destroy all that was good in her.' It is the singer's business to convey the composer's meaning, no doubt. Only, no two singers ever perceive that meaning and express it in exactly the same way, and the difference between a mediocre singer and a great one is likely very largely to lie in the quality of the latter's perception and his ability to convey it to the minds of others. Unless there is something within you, something God-given planted deep in your nature which has to come out, and which you alone can give to your fellows because nobody else has exactly the same thing to give, what excuse have you for inflicting your poor little self upon the world?

VI

And yet she to whom Nature had given all this, and whose gifts had been recognized more widely and greeted with more passionate adoration than those of any other singer of her time, voluntarily left the operatic stage and all that goes with it behind her at the age of twenty-nine. It was when she was at the very height of her European successes that she determined

70

to leave the theater as soon as possible, and once
the determination has been formed, she recurs
to it again and again in language whose passionate intensity leaves no reasonable doubt of
the ardor of her longing for freedom.[79] This is,
of course, no isolated phenomenon in the history of the theater, though perhaps no other
abdication was ever quite so splendid as hers.
Mary Anderson retired at thirty: though she is
still very much alive, one must, as it were, make
an effort to realize her presence, and her
achievements belong to the theater of the past
quite definitely as do those of Adelaide Neilson,
who has been in her grave these fifty years.
Somewhat closer to Jenny Lind's experience
has been that of Olive Fremstad, an artist
whose attainments only a few years ago were
not surpassed in kind by any singer of her time,
and who has now passed into permanent retirement where one hopes she may have found in
other interests a deeper contentment and satisfaction than her great art was ever able to give
her. And only within the last few years, we
have had the case of the charming Miss Marion
Talley, who, like Jenny Lind, seems to have
found small personal satisfaction in her operatic
successes, though in this case there are indica-

71

tions also that retirement was rather more alluring in prospect than it was in actual experience. And then, by way of contrast, we have, at
the other extreme, such amazing creatures as
Sarah Bernhardt and Robert B. Mantell. Age
could not dim their enthusiasm. Illness and in-
jury could not force their sun down before its
time. Both of them virtually died on the stage,
giving to the end, spending the last breath they
had in their bodies in the service of their art,
powerless apparently to throw off the harness or
to find satisfaction in any other pursuit whatever.

Taken all in all, renunciation has probably
been a sadly overrated virtue in this world, yet
it would be hazardous to assume that Jenny
Lind who gave up the stage at twenty-nine was
less sincere in her devotion to her art, or that
she had probed less deeply into its treasures
than had Sarah Bernhardt, who was nearly
eighty when death ended her and her career
together. To be sure, Jenny Lind's was not an
absolute retirement, like Mary Anderson's. All
her life she continued to sing in concert more or
less, though in later years her appearances became more and more infrequent. But she did
not lose her interest in music. Even after her

own singing days were definitely over, much of
her time and strength went into teaching and
the various problems of musical education. I
have no definite evidence which enables me to
say positively that a desire to sing better music
than the operatic repertoire generally afforded
was one of the motives that led her to leave the
stage, yet, being the creature we know she was,
it were vain to suppose that an eternity of 'La
Sonnambula' and 'Lucia' and 'La Figlia' could
permanently have satisfied her spirit. Sooner
or later she must have taken the step she took,
must have passed on to Bach and the great
oratorios.

To be sure, though Jenny Lind retired early,
her career in the theater — as distinguished
from her operatic career, strictly speaking —
covered a period of nineteen years. It may well
be that had she entered upon theatrical life at a
less early age, she might not have wearied of it
almost as soon as she had entered her prime.
Mary Anderson once remarked that she gave
up the stage because she was tired of the grease-
paint. I suppose she meant what her friend
Henry James meant when, after the failure of
his attempt as a playwright, he was driven to
the distinction which most sensitive people come

73

sooner or later to make with him, saying that while he loved the drama he hated the theater. In her early years, however, Jenny did not hate even the theater. She loved it, loved it with a love that was strong enough to overcome the pious, middle-class Swedish prejudice against it. To her father she wrote from Paris in 1842: 'I wonder when I shall next be allowed to see myself "on the boards," as the term is. I clearly see — yes, I do see, Papa — that I am born to stand on them.' [80] And to another correspondent she had written: 'Oh! to pour out my feelings in a beautiful part! This is, and ever will be, my continual aim; and, until I stand there again, I shall not know myself as I really am. Life on the stage has in it something so fascinating, that I think, having once tasted it, one can never feel truly happy away from it, especially when one has given oneself wholly up to it, with life and soul, as I have done.' [81]

To be sure, she early recognized the hollowness of popular triumph, the lack of real warmth and appreciation in popular applause. And this she might well be expected to have done, for no human being was ever the object of more vulgar adulation, more ill-mannered curiosity than she. 'Where, then,' she asks — and every

74

intelligent artist of today will echo the cry —
'Where, then, is there more than a little nucleus
that feels anything sincerely, or honestly re-
joices about *anything at all?* ' [82] Even when the
clamor was loudest, it often seemed hollow in
her ears. 'It is not me they admire, but my
voice; and that cannot make me happy, though
it gives them delight.' [83] Sometimes the very
force, the intensity of their admiration disgusted
her: 'I have appeared twice in Norma, and was
called so many times before the curtain that I
was quite exhausted. Bah! I do not like it.
Everything should be done in moderation;
otherwise it is not pleasing.' [84] Yet she felt the
seduction of applause as well: she could not have
been human otherwise. Sometimes she quite
openly exults in it. 'What a position I have now
attained! All the musical talent of Europe is, so
to speak, at my feet. What great things has the
Almighty vouchsafed me!' [85] And as late as the
time of her début in London, long after she had
decided to retire, the old thrill was still there.
'Yesterday… I made my first appearance here
… and it went *so*, that, through the whole night,
I could not sleep, for joy!' [86]

Jenny Lind's attitude toward herself as artist
is an interesting and a complicated matter. It

75

is evident that she suffered terribly from stage-
fright. And this not only when critically important engagements were in question. Small
assemblies were, if possible, even worse for her:
once she broke down completely while singing
'Auf Flügeln des Gesanges' at a private party
in London.[87] The phenomenon, while in its
extreme form rare among great artists, is by no
means unknown. Richard Mansfield suffered
from it to the end of his life, every performance
being a dreaded ordeal, to be prepared for long
hours in advance; and one of the most famous
prima donnas of today had literally to be pushed
out onto the stage the night of her first appearance at the Metropolitan Opera House. Jenny
Lind was in a mood of hopeless despondency
preceding her Berlin début. She looked forward
with dread to her engagement in Vienna, and
when she arrived and saw the auditorium there,
she was so sure her voice could not fill it that she
wanted to cancel her engagement. Mansfield
often trembled, but he went resolutely ahead.
Jenny Lind often did nothing of the kind, and
had it not been for the loving and encouraging
advices by which she was always surrounded,
she would probably have had a very unimpor-
tant career. There was a kind of artistic miser-

76

liness about her in this connection, or at least a kind of excessive caution. She was so afraid of losing what she held that she would not open her hands to reach out for more. 'And yet — only think! — what if I lose my whole reputation!' [88] 'It is not a question of money, but simply of my existence as an artist, which would be compromised by my appearance in London, and perhaps annihilated by my *début* at Drury Lane.' [89] Her loyal friend Meyerbeer was so seriously troubled by this tendency in Jenny Lind that he ventured to remonstrate with her upon the subject, praying for her relief 'from those doubts in the power of your talent which turn even your days of triumph into days of anxiety; the removal of that indecision and irresolution which throw you into such continual agitation; and, finally, the disappearance of that diffident temperament, which, rendering you distrustful of the source of the sympathies you inspire, may perhaps, in the end, deprive you of that most beautiful consolation of human life, friendship.' [90]

But it was in connection with the long and complicated negotiations preceding her London début that this hesitancy of Jenny Lind's was most strikingly manifested, and as one follows

77

the record here, one begins to wonder a bit concerning her emotional stability. Her admirers have all taken it for granted that she was perfectly justified in breaking the contract with Alfred Bunn which called for her début at Drury Lane; but Bunn's own cool, objective account of the controversy, in his pamphlet, 'The Case of Bunn versus Lind,' makes it clear enough that there is another side to the matter. When she declared she could not master the English language in time for her proposed début, he offered to permit her to sing in either German or Italian instead. When she wished to pay him £2000 to be released from her contract, he agreed to accept, provided she would sing three times at Drury Lane before she sang anywhere else in England. Finally he professed himself ready to give up even these performances if she would furnish 'written assurance, that you were not deterred from appearing on the Drury Lane stage by any other motive than the one assigned in your letter of the 17th of October, 1845, wherein, on asking me to cancel our agreement, you offered me an ample indemnification should you ever appear at her Majesty's Theatre. I make this final proposal to you,' the letter went on, 'to restore our former good understanding, to avoid further litigation, and to dispense with any more public discussion.' This communication Jenny Lind did not see fit to answer, whereupon Bunn took legal action and won his case. It would certainly seem that he had tried to meet her a good deal more than halfway. And what is even more to the point is that she came very near going through the same comedy when she was engaged by Benjamin Lumley for Her Majesty's. Even after she had actually come to London for the purpose, she was afraid to appear, and for a long time she did not do so. Indeed, hopes for her appearance had been well-nigh given up and discussion had been dropped when, at last, upon hearing that the opera business was at a standstill and Mr. Lumley losing money every day, she decided suddenly to take the plunge. And then she chose 'Roberto il Diavolo' for her début, because it would give her a chance to make her first entrance on a crowded stage and have time to collect her faculties before she should be called upon to sing.[91]

Yet Jenny Lind was not devoid of personal ambition. Her more fanatical admirers have, of course, always denied this, but the evidence is against them. She was, indeed, a severe critic

79

of her own work, and her extreme conscientiousness would not permit her to accept gracefully
any suffrages that she did not feel she had fairly
earned. It was this consideration that led her
to Garcia. 'I am gifted by Nature; and to that
I am indebted for a certain amount of success;
but Art I did not know, even by name. I felt
this bitterly; and it made me receive the applause of the public with sorrow rather than
with joy: for I felt that I did not deserve it.' [92]
And Hans Christian Andersen tells how, when
she was received with enthusiasm at Copenhagen, her response was to retire to a corner
alone and weep. 'Yes, yes, I will exert myself,
I will endeavor; I will be better qualified than
I am when I again come to Copenhagen.' [93]

She did exert herself, for Art and for God, no
doubt, but she felt the sting of competition while
she was about it, and she would not have been
human if she had not exerted herself also for
Jenny Lind. To be sure, she was never involved in conflicts with other singers, the kind
of conflict that enlivened Adelina Patti's career.
In Berlin, in 1844, when she learned that
another singer considered herself entitled to
the rôle in 'Das Feldlager in Schlesien' which
Meyerbeer had designed for her, she immedi-

ately relinquished it, though, indeed, she makes it clear that her desire to avoid unpleasant conflict and her comparative unfamiliarity, at this time, with the German language, were the motives which inspired her act, much more than the mere desire to be generous to Fräulein Tuczec.[94] But the real sting came closest to her when she was called upon to measure her gifts alongside those of Henrietta Nissen, who was to her what Breslau was to Marie Bashkirtseff.

Nissen, like Jenny Lind, was a pupil of Garcia's, and she had some obvious gifts which Jenny lacked. Jenny felt they were distinctly of the superficial variety, and it hurt her to think that Garcia did not see the difference between herself and her rival quite so clearly as she thought he ought to see it. On one occasion, when she and Nissen sang together in Stockholm, the newspapers found it somewhat difficult to decide which was the finer singer.[95] Indeed, for a time Nissen seemed to be making better progress than Lind. 'I am not depressed on Mademoiselle Nissen's account. Ah, no! Besides, how foolish it would be not to stand aside for a merit greater than my own — and this I do. Thank God! I feel no jealousy, and — shall I tell you? — it is true that I can never

81

get her voice; but I am quite satisfied with my own. And, furthermore, I shall be able, in time, to learn all that she knows; but she can never learn what I know. Do you understand? She is a nice girl; and, with all my heart, I wish her every happiness. Her stay here is of great advantage to me, for she spurs me on.' [96] And again, 'Should there be any who think it worth while to envy me, how contented will they not be, when they see me quietly disembark at the Stockholm Skeppsbro, while Nissen will soon be *prima donna*. I do not understand how it is that this takes no effect upon me!'[97]

But when it came to returning to Stockholm, there were other factors and other personalities to consider, and we find her writing the officials of the Royal Theater with this consideration in mind.'... I shall certainly return, in a year and a half — quite certainly — but, not if I meet with coldness, or am regarded as altogether unnecessary. I am almost afraid of that. Elma Ström has everything in her favour, which I have against me. She has a much softer and better voice to work with than I ever had, during the whole time of my working period. She ought, therefore, to sing very well. The actress, probably, will come later on. I do not wish to

stand in her way, or in the way of any one.
Rather than that, I would settle down here to
give singing-lessons; for Garcia's method is the
best of our time, and every one, here, is striving
to follow it.' [98] Note the delicious condescen-
sion, the quite human reservation: 'She ought,
therefore, to sing very well. The actress, probably, will come later on.' It does not sound
very much like the singer who did not know
worldly ambition and who sang only for God.

VII

Of her ability as an actress, Jenny Lind was
if anything more self-confident than she was as
a singer. Except for the early training in
Stockholm, she was practically self-taught here,
and she always felt that she had made a pretty
good job of it. 'With regard to my acting,' she
writes from Paris in 1842, 'I can compete with
any one here. But, there are many other things
that I lack.' [99] She goes so far, this girl of
twenty-two, as to compare herself with Rachel.
'The difference between Mademoiselle Rachel
and myself is, that she can be splendid when
angry, but she is unsuited for tenderness. I am
desperately ugly, and nasty too, when in anger;
but I think I do better in tender parts.' And

83

then, bethinking herself suddenly, she adds somewhat mawkishly, 'Of course, I do not compare myself with Rachel. Certainly not. She is immeasurably greater than I. Poor me!' [100] When she came to London and heard a performance of 'I Puritani,' she whispered to Mrs. Grote who was her companion, 'I think I can do as well as that, and perhaps a little better.' [101] Sometimes her satisfaction in minor aspects of her art has even an attractive touch of childlike pleasure in it, as when she writes of Signor Battaglia, after her London début, '... tell him that my Italian pronunciation has been so successful, that Lablache was quite astonished at it.' [102] And again she writes to friends, as summing up her well considered judgment, 'I feel, now, better than I used to do what life really is. It is just possible that I may not act as well as before; but I do not think so. Nobody acts as I act. What do you say to such language as this? But you will not misunderstand me.' [103]

This exalted estimate of herself — her own character and her powers — naturally did not tend to diminish as she grew older, and it finds perhaps its best expression in the precious letter she wrote in 1865 to the editor of the Swedish 'Biografiskt Lexicon.' 'For me,' she said, 'mankind, in general, has done very little. I never was in want of anything, and asked help of no one.' 'As to the greater part of what I can do in my art, I have myself acquired it by incredible work, and in spite of astonishing difficulties; it is from Garcia alone that I learned some few important things. To such a degree had God written within me what I had to study. My ideal was (and is) so high, that no mortal could be found who, in the least degree, could satisfy my demands; therefore I sing after no one's "methode" — only after that of the birds (as far as I am able); for their Teacher was the only one who responded to my requirements for truth, clearness, and expression....' [104] Yvette Guilbert once remarked that she would not trust her voice to any teacher. It is comforting to know that Jenny Lind trusted God and the birds. She signed this letter 'Humbly and affectionately.' With such things in mind, it is rather difficult to believe in her entire sincerity when, for example, she writes: '...it goes well with me here, as everywhere. I am beginning to feel accustomed to this, though I cannot conceive what it is that satisfies the people.' [105]

I do not mean to leave the impression that Jenny Lind's self-confidence was based on

vanity. She *was* a great artist and a great singer:
had she failed to recognize it, it would be necessary to set her down as a woman of very poor
judgment besides! Every great artist realizes his
greatness, or, if he does not, he fails to take full
advantage of his possibilities. Here Jenny is her
own best defender. 'Perhaps you think that I
have grown vain?' she writes. 'No. God shield
me from that! I know what I can do. I should
be very stupid if I did not. But I know, equally
well, what I cannot do.' [106] At its best, this self-
confidence shows most attractively in what followed when, upon her arrival in Paris, Garcia
told her she had worn out her voice and pre-
scribed six weeks of absolute rest. She followed
his directions scrupulously, but the time was
not wasted. Instead, she spent it in studying
French and Italian, so that when she began to
sing again — as she confidently assumed that
she would — she might use these languages.
Even after she had begun her studies, Garcia
did not understand her full capacities as quickly
as it now seems he might have grasped them,
perhaps not even as quickly as in later years he
came to persuade himself that he had. 'He did
not understand my individuality.' [107] But Jenny
did not accept even his judgment when it came

86

into conflict with her own. 'Then Garcia pretends to believe that I shall never more act in tragic parts! What do you think of that! I leave him to say what he pleases. In the meantime, may God preserve me from being altogether bewildered.' [108]

No more than other artists, however, was Jenny Lind's attitude toward herself calm and unwavering, nor did her performance always come up to her own ideal. Miss Lenore Ulric has remarked that a woman who is to win success as an actress must be satisfied that she can do anything in the theater, but she must never be satisfied with anything she does. Jenny Lind understood the formula perfectly. After she had sung 'Das Feldlager' for the first time, Meyerbeer found her in tears, lamenting that she had ruined his opera. 'I wish,' she once quietly remarked, referring to a very minor singer about the theater, 'I wish I could hope to become, one day, as great an artist, as Fräulein —— believes herself to be every day.' [109] Personally I am much less disturbed over Jenny Lind's expressions of self-confidence than I am over her professions of humility. Frequently these latter have an unconvincing, pietistic flavor about them. One feels that 'the lady doth protest too much,' that she speaks as she does, not from any inner urging, but rather because the good pastors have taught her that humility is one of the Christian virtues. Thus, in 1845, she declined to appear in Paris before what she calls 'the first audience in the world.' 'For,' she says, 'the more I think of it, the more I am persuaded that I am not suited for Paris, nor Paris for me.' [110] And I for one do not believe that she felt the differences between them to be wholly to the credit of Paris. To Alfred Bunn she writes, during the negotiations preceding her English engagement, 'I neither possess the personal advantages, the assurance, nor the charlatanism of other prime donne....' [111] Even Vienna must be approached with caution. 'Herr Pokorny would not be very well pleased, for instance, if I were to sing there once only and, that once, fail. For the money he offers me he can get singers anywhere who are not so difficult to satisfy as I am, and who, at least, wish for something, while I wish for nothing at all!' [112] I think Mr. Werner's sharp comment at this point is perfectly just: 'In this and other letters of a similar character one gets the impression that Jenny Lind was extremely proud of her humility.' [113]

This rather maddening humility of Jenny Lind's — which, of course, was not really humility at all, any more than losing your life in order to find it is genuine self-sacrifice — shows nowhere more interestingly than in the plans she made for her autobiography, the autobiography that never was written. 'My life — especially as an artist — has furnished material for a biography in such abundance, that I almost look upon it as a duty to produce something of the kind, before leaving a world where I had been called upon to take so active a part.' Duty? Is that why people write autobiographies? Listen to Marie Bashkirtseff: 'Of what use were pretense or affectation? Yes, it is evident that I have the desire, if not the hope, of living upon this earth by any means in my power. If I do not die young I hope to live as a great artist; but if I die young, I intend to have my journal, which cannot fail to be interesting, published.' [114] Marie has been censured long enough for her 'egotism.' Is it not better than mock-humility? And that the real motive behind Jenny Lind's projected autobiography — what a document it would have been! — was precisely identical with that which informed Marie's, is clear enough from the sequel.

89

When she gave up the plan, she justified herself by her indignation at the treatment accorded Carlyle's 'Reminiscences.' 'If they could so treat him, who was so great, what respect would they pay me? No! let the waves of oblivion pass over my poor little life!' [115] The claims of 'duty' would seem suddenly to have become somewhat less compelling.

It is notable, too, that hesitant as Jenny Lind was to embark upon an untried enterprise, a challenge to her pride was never allowed to pass unheeded. A. A. Bournonville has told of his amusing experience in persuading her to sing in Copenhagen in 1842. Here she went through all sorts of nervous fears as was her custom. She doubted her ability to cope with a foreign stage; she feared the competition of Fru Heiberg, and so on. She became so excited that she finally accused him of having prepared a trap for her. 'This both frightened and wounded me; and I promised to cancel all. But now the "woman" came to the front; for as I began to doubt, she waxed firm.' [116]

Sometimes her advisers deliberately played upon this tendency. In 1844, after she had studied in Paris, the Royal Theater at Stockholm offered her an engagement for eight years at a salary of five thousand dollars a year, to be continued later as a pension for life. Though her friends strongly urged her not to tie her talents to a single theater, she herself was more than a little inclined to accept this paltry offer. While the question was still hot, one of her friends happened to mention the matter to a certain Consul-General who set himself up as an authority on music, and who replied at once that she was wise, since her powers would not be equal to a success on the Continent. 'Well knowing the effect which this absurd misrepresentation... could not fail to produce upon Jenny's mind, her friend lost no time in making her acquainted with it; and then and there he had the satisfaction of seeing her tear up the fatal contract and thus put an end to the discussion for ever.' [117]

But Jenny Lind's strength and weakness as an artist were alike bound up with the much more intricate matter of her strength and weakness as a human being. The singer and the actor, alone among artists, consciously and definitely use themselves as the medium of their art: the instrument upon which they perform is their own body and soul. And in this case, we have already seen, the woman herself was much more intimately and personally involved than is often the case. Many of her personal characteristics have, of course, been revealed in the foregoing consideration of her work. But it is necessary now to turn to the study of her personality as it revealed itself in more general and less restricted aspects.

III
THE WOMAN

She is the only great, unquestioned genius in woman's form that I have ever known, and the more I see her the more I reverence her truth, her purity, her faith in art as the crown and glory of our nature. You should see her face when she speaks of these things.

BAYARD TAYLOR

Madame Goldschmidt was a very uncertain woman. She was kind, generous, and charitable, but she was very narrow in many ways, and most particular as to the character and conduct of people with whom she associated. She was a woman who knew no evil herself, and could not tolerate it in any one else. She had been surrounded all her life by an adulation which was unparalleled. She had a husband who saw everything through her eyes, and considered everything she did and thought infallible.

LADY ST. HELIER
(MARY JEUNE)

CHAPTER III

The Woman

I

'Of all the forms of fame,' remarks Richard LeGallienne, 'that of Beauty is the greatest, for it is not the fame of achievement, of which one can trace the beginnings and follow the development, but it is the fame of a miracle.' [1] It is, however, a form of fame that Jenny Lind had to manage to get along without. Physical beauty was a thing she had never possessed, and she knew it well. She will not allow herself even the endearing graces of childhood: she was 'a small, ugly, broadnosed, shy "gauche," altogether undergrown girl.' [2] The broad nose remained with her in later years, and she had also the extremely high cheek-bones, the wide, frank, open features so often characteristic of the Swedes. Once a German inquired of her concerning the beauty of Swedish women. 'All the Swedes are beautiful,' she replied. 'It is seldom that one sees anyone like me.' [3] And when the Bournonvilles brought up the much-mooted matter of her refusal to sing in Paris, she said, 'I am too ugly. With my potato nose, it is impossible for me to have any success in Paris.' 4

She was of medium height — five feet, five inches — though it is said she appeared taller. In her Berlin days, an observer who saw her first sitting at the piano before a private concert was able to discern only 'a thin, pale, plain-featured girl.' 5 Frederick Locker-Lampson pronounced her 'a fair-haired and blue-eyed Puritan — an excellent woman, with serious enthusiasms and a plain but impressive personality.' 6 But when Lillie de Hegermann-Lindencrone first saw her in 1866, she found her 'neither handsome nor distinguished-looking; in fact, quite the contrary: plain features, a pert nose, sallow skin, and very yellow hair.' 7

John Addington Symonds is more specific. He met her first in 1862, when she was forty-two and he was twenty years younger. 'She was quite in black, and looked to me an old worn lady with a large head and a small person. She wore no crinoline, and her dress with its loose waist reminded me of grandma's.' He goes on to a careful description of her physiognomy: 'First, the face is terribly thin and worn. The eyes are small, and very glaucous grey. They soon screw up when she looks attentive. The

JENNY LIND AT THE PIANO
By J. Ashton

nose is immense and broad at the base. The mouth broad, and lips thin, with the skin about it pink and irritable. Her hair is profuse, and yellow. Her throat is immense, with a huge larynx. The whole face is mobile and expressive.' [8]

The deficiencies that Nature had left in her were never covered up through skillful dressing, for the subject of clothes was one that did not greatly interest her. Even her friends acknowledged and lamented her carelessness in this regard. 'She was never a good dresser,' remarks her daughter, 'and selected materials more for their quality than for their beauty.' [9] One night she started out for a ball with the Bournonvilles, and her appearance was distinctly shabby. At the last moment Mrs. Bournonville begged her at least to put on a few bracelets. She complied without protest, then turned to her friend. 'How is it now?' she asked indifferently. [10] The same unconcern appears in another aspect in Parker Willis's complaint that she allowed 'with careless willingness, painters and Daguerrotypists to make what they will of her.' [11] When she did sometimes burst forth in gorgeous attire, her taste does not seem always to have been good. On one occasion she is spoken of as wearing four large gold rings on the middle and one on the third finger.[12] And once a visitor who called upon her at eleven o'clock in the morning found her 'dressed in a white brocade trimmed with a piece of red silk around the bottom, a red, blousy waist covered with gold beads sewed fantastically over it, perhaps odds and ends of old finery, and gold shoes!' [13]

Jenny Lind's admirers have never claimed beauty for her: what they do claim is that her features were extraordinarily transparent, expressive, and alive. 'When she smiled,' says Madame de Hegermann-Lindencrone, 'which was not often, her face became almost handsome.' [14] Longfellow said, 'There is something very fascinating about her; a kind of soft wildness of manner, and sudden pauses in her speaking, and floating shadows over her face.' [15] The unusual mobility of her features appears also in the careful description of that keenest of observers, the Reverend J. B. Mozley: 'She had two great powers in her face; one of stiffening it, and the other of resolving it, so to speak; I mean of imparting all sorts of active expressions, chiefly of the arch and comical sort, to it. It was sometimes so perfectly motionless and stiff as to be almost corpse-like, but not without a certain grandeur, an expression of determined obstinacy, stubbornness, and hauteur. Then when she changed to active expression, she had all sorts of odd uses of her eyes, looking from underneath and from the corners of her eyes, and so on, and was certainly excessively arch; and one expression chased another just like waves over the sea.' [16]

But if she did not have beauty, she did have something else which is often immeasurably more valuable to one who bids for the suffrages of the public — that certain irresistible wistful pathos that goes straight to the heart, sometimes altogether supplies the place, and in other cases powerfully supplements the appeal, of different, perhaps higher, gifts. Possibly the best statement is that of Mrs. Price Newman, who heard Jenny Lind when herself a schoolgirl in Nashville, Tennessee, and whose utterance may therefore be taken as in some degree representative of the impression she made, not on the critics, but on the less sophisticated hearers who made up the great body of her audiences. 'There was always a pathos about Jenny Lind. Under all circumstances it remained with her.' [17] And Mrs. Newman's testimony does not stand alone by any means: observer after

99

observer speaks of the same characteristic. For some her wistfulness seemed even to invade her voice: 'The dream-like echoes of the notes still linger in my ear; it was something unearthly — far away; like the cry of a wild bird lost in the sunset.' [18]

Sir James M. Barrie, who should know if any one does, has defined charm as 'a sort of bloom on a woman. If you have it, you don't need to have anything else; and if you don't have it, it doesn't much matter what else you have.' The pathetic look is charm, no doubt, but it is charm in a highly specialized and immensely subtle form. William Webster Ellsworth has related in his delightful book, 'A Golden Age of Authors' how when he first read Irvin S. Cobb he felt somewhat reluctant to admit a new humorist among his old favorites; 'then he wrote "Boys Will Be Boys" and I took him in and fed him and gave him a place to sleep.' [19] In the theater certainly many persons' favorites are those whom they feel they would like to take in and feed and give a place to sleep. Pathos and helplessness appeal profoundly to the protective instinct: they are helpful to the actress in her appeal to men and to women alike.

Then, too, it is extremely difficult to say just

100

where the pathetic and the wistful shades off into the spiritual. Jenny Lind, as we shall see, herself felt a certain connection between sadness and spirituality. In recent years all our emphasis has been placed on the idea that true spirituality means health and joy. We may be right, yet there is something to be said on the other side. Life is a tragedy as well as a comedy, and the richest, most fully rounded natures have always been those, like Shakespeare, like Cervantes, like Molière, who are sensitive enough and brave enough to embrace it in both manifestations. In any case, treat the pathetic look as you will, regard it as purely a physical accident or attribute worlds of spiritual significance to it, the fact remains that Jenny Lind had it and that it played an important part in her career, as it has in that of others. Lotta seems to have possessed it; so does Annie Russell. More recently it has profoundly influenced the response of the public to artists so diverse and so unequal as Maude Adams, Laurette Taylor, Mary Pickford, Mitzi, Rosetta Duncan, Janet Gaynor, and Clara Bow.

The most interesting thing about this whole matter of Jenny Lind's appearance, however, is the extraordinary change that is said to have come over her features when she sang. Testimony here is abundant: many eye-witnesses tell us that, although she was somewhat disappointing when she first stepped on the stage, as soon as she began to sing she was transfigured: she almost seemed another woman. Mrs. Newman describes the change with special reference to her interpretation of 'I Know That My Redeemer Liveth.' 'The pale face became a little more pale, the rather wide mouth became peaceful, the eyes glowed with calm intensity as they raised themselves to the Heaven whence [*sic!*] her soul had ascended.   She was translated to the beyond and chanted with the angels her credo of faith.' But more experienced, less impressible observers can serve us better here than Mrs. Newman. When Lord Broughton heard her as Amina, he 'was charmed beyond measure, not only with her singing but her acting, and forgot her plainness.' [20] Symonds speaks of another occasion when she did not have the accouterments of the stage to assist her: 'As she sat there singing, she became beautiful, and her profile seemed really classical.' [21] Most important of all is her own observation in this connection, 'I become a different thing when I sing — different body, different soul.' [22] When a woman who is not physically beautiful is able to convey a sense of beauty to the mind, then indeed she is an artist — and a personality.

II

Her health was no better than it should have been. Toward the close of her operatic period, her nerves were in a bad state: she suffered continually from frightful neuralgic headaches, and for days after a performance of 'Norma' she was good for nothing. 'Yes, I gave too much of myself in my art,' she wrote in later years; 'all my life's strength was on the point of being extinguished.' [23] Indeed, the doctors had begun to talk rest to her as early as 1842, and by 1846 the situation was serious. Naturally the strain of the American tour, with the element of unfamiliarity and the physical discomforts involved in it, did not tend to improve her condition. In 1853, she wrote to a friend that the ordeal of singing in America to 'Barnumish' houses — '(you will understand all I mean with that only word)' — had completely exhausted her.[24] When she was older, she was much harassed with rheumatism.

But all this, I have no doubt, seemed to have been merely a prelude to her real sufferings when, at the end, she was stricken with cancer. Like our own Charlotte Cushman, it was her fate to do battle with this dread scourge, and then, after all, to die of another ailment. The immediate cause of her death, in November, 1887, was apoplexy.[25]

III

Jenny Lind was an intelligent woman, but she was not in any sense an 'intellectual.' Her early education had, as her official biographers express it, been 'quite simple and unscientific,' [26] and she was hardly in a position to put herself through any very rigid intellectual discipline in later years. Like many artists, she experienced perceptions and made deductions rather by swift flashes of intuition than by way of strictly logical processes. This she herself fully realized, and when she was asked to explain her method in singing, she prefaced an extremely intelligent analysis by saying, 'It has always been difficult for me to present *in words* what has been so individual with me, for I have always been guided by a God-given instinct for what is right in Art and on that I have always acted. Such persons are seldom able to explain or offer arguments over what to them is so simple and natural.' [27]

And we are told that, while she was not a con-
versationalist, her talk was full of vivid flashes,
swift glimpses of understanding, none of which
she ever stopped to develop logically or con-
sistently. [28] Parker Willis found that 'her occasional anticipations of the speaker's meaning,
though they had a momentary look of abrupt-
ness, were invariably the mile-stones at which
he was bound to attain.' [29]

In science and in abstract thought, she shows
no interest whatever, and since she found all she
needed to know about God and destiny in the
creed of her church, there was no necessity for
her to engage in metaphysical or philosophical
speculation of any kind. Politics as such did not
interest her either. She was disturbed and depressed by the revolutions of 1848, and she was
rabidly pro-German in the Franco-Prussian
War, but that is all.

Her interest in literature was much greater,
but this, too, was evidently quite haphazard and
unsystematic. Her note from Weimar in 1846
— 'I have just come out of the vault in which
Goethe and Schiller lie entombed, and my
whole heart is impressed and excited' [30] — is too
conventional to tell us much. Later she disliked
Goethe extremely because she thought his in-

fluence had made the Germans irreligious.[31]
She read Hans Andersen's stories as they were
published, read them and wept over them and
praised them extravagantly.[32] She was greatly
moved also when the elder Symonds read Tennyson's 'Guinevere' to her, and she refused
when she was asked to sing after he had finished.
'The vibrations will clash,' [33] she said. 'Uncle
Tom's Cabin' made, as might have been expected, a pronounced humanitarian appeal to
her.[34] On the other hand, I find myself quite
unable to understand her dislike of Sir Walter
Scott, whose novels, she declared, did her soul
no good.[35]

It is interesting, too — and from my stand-
point a little amusing — to find that she disliked biography, disliked it because it reveals
the faults of great men. 'What good can we get
from seeing how Bacon fell? Ah, that did give
me pain. I would sooner have known evil of
some near friend.' [36] So the cold Sir Francis
Bacon, the wily serpent of Lytton Strachey's
brilliant pages, dead more than two hundred
years, still woke a sympathetic throb of pain in
a Swedish heart! But oh! what would she say to
modern biographies! And what in the world
would she say to this one!

As soon as Jenny Lind can connect literature with music, it is astonishing how quickly she reveals a keen, incisive critical faculty. Thus she had decided convictions on what sort of poetry might successfully be set to music. Milton, Dryden, and Heine were all suitable for this purpose, but Shakespeare, Shelley, and Tennyson were far too complex. One harmony, one feeling was what the composer needed, not a series of broken lights. 'Tennyson takes all the solid sharp words and puts them together. Music cannot come between. He does not flow.' [37]

In the theater she had always a more or less professional interest, and she thrilled to good performances, especially in her younger days.[38] In 1871, she was profoundly stirred by the Passion Play at Oberammergau, though she afterwards declared that 'the most holy scenes the world has witnessed ought never to be reproduced in a theater.' [39] She was a severe critic of theatrical performances, but she retained her interest and her faith in the theater itself as long as she lived.

The art galleries of Dresden and of Florence appealed to her emotions deeply, but she was quite the layman in her observation of pictures.

107

'Papa was asking her about pictures,' writes J. A. Symonds in 1862. 'She admired at Dresden, the great Madonna, Titian's Tribute Money, and Carlo Dolci's Christ Breaking Bread, more than any. "The Madonna," she said, "is not painted — it is thought — it is there — you see it — you cannot call it painted." But of ordinary art-criticism she had none. Simple feeling was all that gave her a preference for one picture over the other.' [40]

I find only one suggestion of her taste in the matter of architecture, and this, oddly enough, would seem to indicate that she was attracted by the fantastic and the ornate. At least, she tremendously admired that particular example of it that was Barnum's house, 'Iranistan,' a picture of which she saw first on the showman's letter-head. She told Barnum, indeed, that she would never have come to America if it had not been for 'Iranistan.' 'I said to myself, a gentleman who has been so successful in his business as to be able to build and reside in such a palace cannot be a mere "adventurer." ' [41] I am afraid there are some of us who, if we had to decide on the basis of 'Iranistan' alone, would conclude that that was just what he was.

IV

She was a great lover of Nature. 'I believe
the good God did his best, when he raised the
mountains,' [42] she writes; and when she traveled
through Switzerland, she was tremendously
impressed by their beauty, the majestic com-
mentary they made on the petty pride of man. [43]
When she crossed the Atlantic, the ever-chang-
ing moods of the ocean was a subject of endless
fascination to her. [44] But it was by no means
only the spectacular or the theatrical aspects of
Nature that appealed to her. She had spent the
first four years of her life in the country, and
though she was always in the city thereafter, the
impressions thus early implanted did not wear
off. She loved birds and water and flowers —
wild flowers, not cultivated gardens. She felt
most at home among peasants, and she loathed
the city, with its dirt, its crowds, and its excitement. 'Our Jenny recruits herself daily,' writes
her mother, during a rest period in 1839, 'now
in the hay-stacks, now on the sea or in the
swing, in perfect tranquillity....' [45] Once with
some friends she was engaged in watching a
nightingale. Observing his observers, the bird
suddenly stopped singing. 'There!' she exclaimed, 'he has seen us! Now that is just like

me. I should have done the same, if I had
caught anyone intruding on my solitude. And,
indeed, those who compared me to the nightingale were not far wrong; for I have a great
deal of the nightingale in me.' [46]

Naturally, since she had first learned to love
Nature in Sweden, the Swedish aspects of natural beauty might have been expected always
to hold a special charm for her. And this is
what her Swedish patriotism was: a love of
home, a loyalty to the associations of formative
years. It implied no political attachment whatever, and there was never any vulgar flag-
waving in connection with it. Indeed, her
patriotism and her art were all mixed up together. As late as 1868 she was of the opinion
that 'Scandinavian voices have a charm which
no other voices in the whole world have.' She
attributes it to the natural beauty of their
country. But, she at once adds with fine honesty, instruction is miserable in Sweden, and
the strange, contrasted slowness and excitability
of the national temperament is a great handicap.[47] After she first went abroad, she suffered
terribly from homesickness, but when she returned from her study in Paris, she was much
disturbed by the unrest she found in her native

country, then just beginning to hear the echoes
of the general European revolutionary movement.[48] And once she had seen England,
Sweden seems somewhat to have declined in
her estimation. France she loathed always, and
blamed French influence for the distasteful
change in her own country, but there was no
patriotic animus involved: it was simply that
the French point of view and her own would
not go together. Indeed, I think the only thing
she ever really found out about France was that
Paris is a wicked city. Once in her life she did
yield to the charm of a Parisian spring.[49] But
that was a moment of weakness: her real attitude comes out in an 1849 letter, when she
says, 'I don't know whether you can understand my miserable English, but I prefer to
write ever so bad English than the very best
French!' [50] So, while in the deepest sense she
was always loyal to Sweden — 'One's heart is
in one's own country, and mine, certainly, is
Swedish to the very backbone of my body and
soul' [51] — the charms of England grew upon
her more and more in her later years, and
it was in England finally that she made her
home.

V

Neither Jenny Lind's faults nor her virtues
were such as to fit her supremely for social success. Was it Disraeli who said of Gladstone that
he was a man without a single redeeming vice?
Jenny Lind's pride, her severity, her impulsive-
ness, her uncertain temper were vices, no doubt,
but they were not the sort of vices that endear
one to a hostess. When she was on a concert-
tour, she once astonished her companions by
carefully stopping up her ears with wool before
retiring for the night, in order — she said — to
shut out the noises of the world.[52] There are
times when the action almost seems symbolic
of her whole social attitude. 'In later years,'
writes her daughter, 'there was a sense of aloof-
ness and almost haughtiness with those who
were not her friends, this attitude giving offence
to intruders on her private life whose visits she
resented, and Mr. Goldschmidt had to use all
his inherent powers of tact and diplomacy to
put things right again.'[53] But it was not only
in later years that this tendency was manifested,
though undoubtedly it grew upon her with the
passing of time. Even Hans Andersen, who
afterwards became such a close friend, was received 'distantly, almost coldly,' when he first

JENNY LIND IN PHILADELPHIA IN 1850

called upon her in her youth. 'I had,' he writes, 'the impression of a very ordinary character which soon passed away from my mind.' [54]

When Jenny Lind was first received into 'society,' the novelty and the glamour of it rather charmed her. But the spell did not last long. She had, indeed, the Old World deference for rank and position. When she was staying with the Bishop of Norwich, she never spoke to either her host or his wife until one or the other had first spoken to her, nor did she ever sit down with them until invited to do so.[55] Yet the independence of the artist was hers also, and when, upon her arrival in London, Queen Victoria invited her to come and sing at the palace, she very calmly excused herself on the ground that she must save her strength against her début at the opera house on the following night.[56] Jenny Lind's friends have always insisted that even her social failings were the direct result of some of her finest qualities. It can hardly be denied that a large share of social intercourse consists of polite hypocrisy, the genteel expression of feelings that you do not possess and that nobody supposes you to possess. Well, Jenny Lind always cared a great deal more for honesty than she did for politeness, and petty hypocrisies were not for her. 'If a remark is made which has no rebound in it, she drops it with a monosyllable, and without ever gracing its downfall with an insincere smile. She affects no interest which she does not feel; and puts an abrupt end to a conversation which could only be sustained by mutual pretence of something to say; she differs suddenly and uncompromisingly when her sense of truth prompts her to do so; and repels, instead of even listening silently to, complimentary speeches.' [57] DeWolf Hopper has related engagingly how he once tried to 'gush' to Mrs. Fiske, only to have her remark, 'Thanks so much; let us change the subject.' Well, that is not the easiest sort of woman to get on with, but by the time you have met seven or eight thousand charming hostesses who have schooled themselves into such perfect amiability that they have not experienced an honest reaction in twenty years, you may come to feel that there is something to be said for the Jenny Lind or Mrs. Fiske method.

Sometimes her frankness went so far as to be amusing, as when she told a fashionable hostess to her face that she pitied her because she had too much money. [58] When the Mayor of Boston greeted her with a fervent address in praise of her 'character,' she interrupted him sharply: 'What do you know of my private character? What *can* you know of my private character? Sir, I am no better than other people, no better.' [59] And once, when she suspected Horace Greeley of tricking her at a *séance* they attended together, she suddenly called across the table to him, 'in the tone and manner of an indifferently bold archduchess,' peremptorily commanding him to take his hands from under the table, and poor Greeley, who was quite incapable of such trickery, was so nonplussed that he did not know what to make of her. [60]

Like the rest of us, she seems to have allowed her social attitude to be governed largely by her moods. Once the officials of a convent to which she had made a donation came to her in state: a procession of children, banners, robes, and ten or twelve priests. 'I will not see them,' she said; 'they have nothing to thank me for. If I have done good, it is no more than my duty, and it is my pleasure. I do not deserve their thanks, and I will not see them.' [61] But when a poor old Italian dancer whom she had helped wanted to call on her and bring his performing dog along with him, she was so touched that she wept. 'Poor man, poor man,' she said to Barnum, 'do let him come; it is all the good creature can do for me. I like that, I like that; do let the poor creature come and bring his dog. It will make him so happy.' [62]

Her complete indifference to the pleasures of the table did not contribute anything to Jenny Lind's social success either. She liked Swedish *Knäckerbröd;* 'herrings and potatoes — a clean wooden-chair, and a wooden-spoon to eat milk-soup with —' [63] that was her idea of a good meal, and nothing bored her more than being compelled to sit at table after she had finished eating. Symonds described her table manners: 'holds her knife *à l'Allemande,* cuts up her meat, and eats it with a fork, rests her knife on a piece of bread.' [64] With regard to the use of wines and liquors, she seems to have been far ahead of her time. Clara Schumann tells us that 'she drinks neither wine, nor tea, nor coffee — in every respect she is an ethereal being!' [65] Barnum's testimony conflicts here, for according to his account, Jenny was preparing to pledge him in a glass of wine when, to her great surprise, he informed her that he was a teetotaler and would be obliged to drink her health in a glass of cold water.[66] But Barnum is not always a reliable witness, and Madame Schumann's statement does harmonize with and explain an otherwise puzzling incident in young Edouard Brockhaus's account of a celebration in Jenny's honor in 1845. When a bowl of champagne was brought to her, with the request that she taste it and then pass it round to the gentlemen, she refused, 'why, I cannot imagine,' adds the boy. 'She passed it on, however, to David, saying, "Drink to your own health!"' [67]

To be sure, this matter of social success was complicated in her case by the fact that she was a celebrity. She always resented being an object of curiosity at social gatherings, and she was furiously indignant when she discovered that she had been invited as a friend when what her hostess really desired was that she should sing for the other guests. Sometimes when she was asked to sing under such circumstances, she flatly refused,[68] though she rejoiced to sing freely for those of her friends who had not laid a trap for her.[69] Indeed, when she was in good spirits she would sing anywhere, as once at a hotel in Garmisch, and on such occasions the assistance and coöperation of the persons about her would be 'commanded' in the style of a queen giving orders to her obedient subjects.[70]

One evening, Lady St. Helier and her husband, having made a mistake in the date of their invitation, burst in upon Jenny Lind unexpectedly at dinner time. Said she, magisterially: 'We waited dinner last night for you till nine o'clock, and you did not come. Tonight Madame Schumann is dining with me, and has made it a condition that we shall be absolutely alone. Therefore I cannot ask you to stay to our dinner.' The even-tempered Goldschmidt could not with alacrity embrace such heroic methods. Surely they would be able in some way to provide for their guests! But his strong-minded wife, restating her objections, over-ruled him, and the nonplussed visitors were obliged to depart with as good grace as possible and seek their dinner in a restaurant.[71]

On another occasion, Miss Gaynor Simpson, who was very intimate with Jenny Lind and a frequent guest in her house, asked her to write in an autograph album. The singer rose abruptly. 'Well,' she said, 'I did not think you had been a commonplace person.' And she stalked out of the room into the garden. In a little while she came back, a beautiful rose in her hand as a kind of mute peace offering, and continued the previous conversation. Finally, as the girl rose to leave, she asked suddenly,

'Now, where is your birthday book?' and taking it, quietly wrote her name in it.[72]

If this were her manner with friends, it may easily be imagined what her attitude toward intruders would be. In Charleston, Barnum told her of a wealthy young lady who was so anxious to meet her that she had disguised herself as a servant in the hope of thus gaining access to her. But Jenny was deaf to any suggestion that she receive the girl. No, she said, 'It is not admiration — it is only curiosity, and I will not encourage such folly.' [73] In later years she used to sit in the garden of her house in England with a large red umbrella beside her, and if any bold spirit presumptuously peeped in at the gate, she would instantly shoot the thing open and take refuge behind it.[74] Once some Americans actually succeeded in forcing their way into her drawing-room. Jenny entered, stiff as a poker, and asked them to state their business. Somewhat abashed, they replied that they had simply wanted to see her, to make her acquaintance. 'Well,' said Jenny, 'here is my front!' and she made a profound bow. Then, turning about, 'There is my back. Now, you can go home and say that you have seen me.' With which, abruptly, she left the room. Yet after

they had gone, she was overwhelmed with re-
morse for her rudeness.[75]

Probably she often was, after the outburst
was over and the time had passed by for making
amends. For she was really a sick and much-
harassed woman during these later years. In
her early life, we hear much of her restlessness,
but little is said of any discourtesy or bad temper on her part. Besides, she was an extremely,
an abnormally sensitive person. A single word
would sometimes throw her into painful agitation, and often it cost her a strong effort and
some few minutes' time to conquer her displeasure and once more direct her attention
to the amenities of life. Sir Frederick Pollock
had some first-hand experience of this when he
happened to displease her by expressing his admiration of Scott's novels.[76] One writer says
that on such occasions her eyes would turn green
and her normally benevolent countenance take
on a distinctly hard and formidable look.[77] It
is a damnable kind of temperament to have, and
I suppose the possessor of it deserves even more
sympathy than the victims. But I have no desire to wrest the false cause the right way, or to
find Jenny Lind's thoroughgoing idealism at
the root of all her shortcomings! There is a good

120

deal of sound sense in Lady St. Helier's pronouncement quoted at the beginning of this chapter, and even after all allowances have been made, there still remains something which can be called by no better name than plain bad temper.

One cannot help asking whether there was, beyond this austerity, any underlying or determining stratum of actual melancholy. We have already seen that her stage presence suggested pathos to the minds of others. Her daughter suggests that the uncongenial domestic surroundings of her youth may have had something to do with developing Jenny Lind's marked seriousness of disposition. As an artist she understood joy and had the ability to express it: in 'La Figlia del Reggimento' she communicated a sense of ebullient happiness to her entire audience.[78] And there are times when she expresses joy also in her private capacity. 'I am so glad, so happy, so thankful, that I hardly know what I am doing.' [79] But this is not especially characteristic. What she is much more likely to say is that she knows she ought to be happy; she has her art; she has no right to complain; and so on. At such moments she seems to echo the curious — and bitterly pessimistic

— statement of Stevenson's, that there is no duty we so much underestimate as the duty of being happy. 'When I am alone, you have no idea how different I am — so happy, yet so melancholy that tears are rolling down my cheeks unceasingly.' [80] She was not melancholy in the Edwin Booth sense, not wrapped in Hamlet-like speculative gloom, never oppressed with the feeling that she was carrying the burden of the sins of the world. Yet she was capable of being thrown into profound depression even by some sorrow quite external to herself, like the sudden death of Madame Catalani, of cholera, which occurred in Paris in 1849, when Jenny herself fled the city and which haunted her terribly. And sometimes her sadness was more deeply rooted still: she could not trace it to any definite cause. She had been born with the conviction that life is a serious business, as no doubt it is. Only some of us are able to forget it now and then. She never could for long. And if the wise old saying of Koheleth, 'Be not righteous over much; neither make thyself over wise: why shouldest thou destroy thyself?' would have seemed to her — as I suspect it would, though it was enclosed within the covers of her beloved Bible — impious and shocking, she could certainly have appreciated another saying from the same chapter, 'For as the crackling of thorns under a pot, so is the laughter of a fool.' [81] She would not have had it otherwise. Once, when she was called upon to write a friendly letter to a young boy, she wrote as follows, 'You are just going to begin life, dear Rudolph; and life has quite as much joy as it has sorrow; but I, for my part, prefer the sorrow: for there is something exalted about it, whenever one's heart is full of pain: for then it is that we first feel how poor we are in earth, how rich in heaven.' [82]

VI

But it must not be assumed that Jenny Lind had no humor. Of this, there are many examples. The first Christmas in America, she presented Barnum with a statue of Bacchus in honor of his temperance principles. [83] When Hans Andersen's perpetual wooing became more than ordinarily distasteful, she reminded him of his extreme unlikeness to Apollo by silently handing him a mirror. [84] She used to take a childlike pleasure in showing her treasures to her friends. 'And they all came out of here,' she would say, laughing and pointing to her mouth.[85] After she had attended services in the cathedral at Peterborough, the Dean injudiciously asked her how she had enjoyed the choir. 'Oh, Mr. Dean,' she replied, 'your *cathedral* is indeed most beautiful!' [86] And once when somebody asked her what sort of man George Grote was, she replied, 'Oh! Mr. Grote, he was like a nice old bust in the corner; you could go and dust him!' [87]

It is interesting that her humor did not stop short at herself. Andersen, visiting her in England, found on her sitting-room table a caricature of herself, 'a great nightingale with a girlish face; Lumley was shown putting sovereigns on the tail to get her to sing.' [88] When the singer Lablache declared fervently that her every note was a pearl, she seized his hat, sang into it, and then returned it to him with the observation that she had made him a very wealthy man.[89] But what I like best of all in this connection is her reply to the sentimentalists who asked her what heavenly thoughts had filled her mind when, as Alice in 'Roberto,' she was clinging to the cross. 'I believe,' she said, 'I believe I was thinking of my old bonnet.' [90]

There were times when she had more than humor: she had joy and the gift of merry-

making. There was something childlike about
her, as there often is in very serious people, and
a love of simple things, and this tendency expressed itself naturally and charmingly. She
loved animals also, liked to play with them and
make friends with them, and they were often
in her conversation and her thoughts.[91] Oddly
enough for such a Puritan, she was devoted to
dancing, enjoyed it tremendously herself, and
in later years permitted, encouraged her children to dance, and gave dancing-parties for
them, at which, it is said, many young men
looked forward to a dance with her as a great
honor and a pleasure.[92] Once she and Bournonville settled an argument by dancing a polka.[93]
She even played cards with Sims Reeves when
they were on a concert-tour together.[94] In England, she learned to love horseback-riding; and
when she was in Havana, she played ball on
the lawn of her house, insisted on Barnum playing with her, and teased him about his fatness
and his laziness when he tired too easily. As a
hostess she was assiduous and careful, delighting
to give personal attention to the wants of her
guests.[95] When she went to Oberammergau
with Arthur Coleridge and her husband and
children, she secretly brought a large cold roast

goose along with her from Munich, and glee-
fully served it to them in her bedroom when the
interval came for refreshments.[96] The Passion
Play with cold roast goose! She retained her
gift for mimicry to the end: once she played
a maid in some children's theatricals. 'You see,
I have not lost my old art!' she would exclaim.[97]
And we have one delightful picture of her at a
children's party, 'thumping out the "Swedish
Dance" at the piano...; smiling with joy at the
emphatic rhythm of stamping feet; and then
springing up to dance herself with all the brisk,
bright playfulness of a child....' [98]

Only she could never be thus for long. And
beside the story of the children's party we need
to place Barnum's account of a New Year's Eve
that he and Jenny shared together. Up until a
quarter to twelve she was full of high spirits.
Then suddenly she stopped the festivities.
'Pray let us have quiet; do you see, in fifteen
minutes more, this year will be gone forever!'
And she sat down in silence and rested her head
on her hand.[99] It is a revealing incident, is it
not? And, incidentally, it is very plainly the
action of a woman who is accustomed to leadership in her group.

VII

Jenny Lind's austerity toward the world in general must not be taken to indicate that she did not cherish her friends. Though she was a miserable correspondent, she needed friendship desperately and clung to those she loved with an intimacy that is very appealing. She needed their kind offices, their reassurance, their affection, or she could not live contentedly, at peace with herself. Sometimes her expressions of this dependence sound even a little servile in modern ears. But there can be no question of her entire sincerity. She held back because she would not give herself at all where she could not give herself completely. In 1849, she told Mrs. Stanley that she had no wish to make any more friends: she had enough.[100] How seriously she took the obligations of friendship may be inferred from her saying that it would not be wise for her to make friends while she was in America, 'for I love my friends so dearly that I shall be too unhappy to leave them.'[101] She did not shrink from devoted and intimate offices of friendship: she nursed Arthur Coleridge tenderly when he was ill with ophthalmia; she also once nursed the violinist, Guerini.[102] When Mendelssohn died, she was shaken to the depths — 'everything

127

seemed to me to be dead' — and for two years she could not bring herself to sing his songs.[103] Later, when Ruskin mentioned Mendelssohn to her, she inquired had he known him. 'No.' 'Better for you you did not.' 'How so?' 'The loss — too great.' [104]

In choosing her friends, she was often guided by a kind of blind intuition. This she seems to have trusted implicitly and to have followed wherever it led: once she abruptly left a drawing-room when a woman to whom she had taken an instantaneous dislike walked into it.[105] She was fond of discussing the sympathy of sensitive natures and the magnetic influence they have upon each other.[106] As is often the case with shy or reserved people, when she found a really congenial spirit, there was little formality, and intimacy developed quickly. She found one such in the actor Macready who, so far as the world in general was concerned, was as austere as she was. 'You will wonder that I speak so open to you,' she writes him in 1860, in her broken English, 'although we have seen so little of each other, but I feel that we must well understand each other's way of feeling, and, born with the artistical flame in our hearts, we have wandered through much the same pains and trials, and this makes me to feel no stranger to you, dear Mr. Macready!' [107] But she did not, by any means, confine herself entirely to those who had been born with 'the artistical flame' in their hearts: one of her most intimate friends was Arthur Penrhyn Stanley, later the famous Dean of Westminster, a man who did not know one note from another, and who listened to any music with positive pain.

· It may seem somewhat surprising that Jenny Lind's relations with her mother should have been disturbed by many, not inconsiderable, difficulties. As we have seen, they were separated much during the child's early years, and when she grew up, there was consequently no very strong bond between them. Jenny considered her mother somewhat harsh and unsympathetic: the truth is she was in many ways very much the same kind of woman that Jenny herself became, or rather that she might have become had she lived in her mother's narrow world. In 1834, while she was a pupil at the Royal Theater, she ran away from home, and the theater authorities supported her act. A lawsuit followed at the conclusion of which she was returned to the custody of her parents. But when she was nineteen, she left home for good, and after her return from Paris, she first established her parents comfortably in a house in the country, and then persuaded them to transfer the guardianship at that time required by Swedish law for an unmarried woman from themselves to her friend, Judge Munthe. Nevertheless, she was kind to her mother in the days of her fame, missed her when she was far away from her, especially at the holiday season, and was sincerely grieved over her death. 'My mother's death I have felt most bitterly; everything was now smooth and nice between us; I was in hopes that she would have been spared for many a long year... and that, now that she was quieter and more reasonable, I might have surrounded her old age with joy, and peace, and tender care.' [108] It would be too much to claim that Jenny Lind's relations with her mother add anything to her charm—any more than Charles Dickens's add to his, but she, like him, did her duty and more than her duty, and parents who neglect personally to look after their children while they are young, and then expect to hold them very close in later years, are usually destined to disappointment.

It is very evident that where Jenny Lind gave her friendship, she demanded something in return. Even in her kindnesses, she was likely to be somewhat dictatorial. Sims Reeves said of her: 'Her temper was equal, her feelings always under control. I never knew any one so strict in the observance of self-prescribed rules.' But he soon found that the best way to get on with her was to do as she wished. When they were on tour together, she insisted on his dining with her. He declined on the ground that he wished to spare himself any possible fatigue preceding the concert. Jenny rang for the waiter: 'Place Mr. Reeves's dinner on my table.' she said.[109]

Sometimes, being human, she failed in friendship, as she did finally with Clara Schumann, when they quarreled over Brahms's music, which Jenny loathed, and though there was no actual estrangement, they were never really intimate again. And from Arthur Coleridge she withdrew her favor, without a quarrel, after more than twenty years of friendship, apparently for no better reason than that he had dared to suggest the name of a man she happened to dislike as her husband's successor in an important musical post.

Where a moral question was involved, it is hardly necessary to say that she gave no quarter whatever. She would have no unworthy

friends, for she respected herself, and he who
would enjoy her esteem must be worthy of it.
When she had doubts, she expressed them
frankly. Once, a friend who had indulged in
innuendo in her presence was abruptly shown
the door.[110]

VIII

The subject of friendship brings up a still
greater one — love and marriage. Jenny Lind's
tastes were thoroughly domestic. No more than
Thea Kronborg in 'The Song of the Lark' could
she find satisfaction in art alone. The theory
that in our own day has been advocated by
David Belasco and by Mary Garden — that the
artist should not marry because marriage de-
tracts from his artistic interests and makes it
impossible for him to give undivided attention
to his work — she would have found absurd,
for she was a woman first and an artist afterwards. And she needed the normal surroundings of a woman's life — husband, children,
home. Fame was no substitute for these things.
In early days, lamenting to a friend over the
break-up of a love-affair, she remarks that
though she has many interests, many duties,
'the finest, the most sacred of all — I mean, a

132

mother's love, is forbidden — nay! denied to
me!'[111] And on her American tour, she once
greeted a young mother with the passionate
exclamation, 'Ah! how I envy you! you have
something to live for!' [112] There are several
stories of Jenny Lind's kindliness to children in
the early days, and once when a child burst
into tears over her singing, she was greatly
moved and called it her finest triumph.[113]

There is practically nothing on record concerning Jenny Lind's relations to her own three
children. They came somewhat late in her life,
the first in 1853, when she was thirty-three, and
the youngest in 1861, when she was forty-one.
One would suppose her to have been a rather
austere mother, one who would love her children very deeply, but who would not rest satisfied with anything from them short of the best.
Still, it is difficult to dogmatize: sometimes
those — Richard Mansfield is again an example
— who present the haughtiest exterior to the
world, are the gentlest and most indulgent
within the family circle. There is one rather
amusing story about a governess. Jenny quarreled with her and sent her away. But after the
girl had taken a new place, she decided she
could not get on without her, the successor hav-

ing 'no soul, no heart, no head'; so she swallowed her pride and sent for her again.[114]

As for love, one intimate observer says of her, 'In her own character, she was not a woman to fall in love with; she was too reserved.'[115] In spite of the reserve, several, first and last, seem to have been able to manage it. We may throw out the doubtful cases: Hjortzberg,[116] Lindblad,[117] Josephson, Mendelssohn, and Belletti. There still remain three serious love-affairs, one of which ripened into a happy marriage. Of Belletti, Maunsell B. Field says that he 'used to lie in bed all day, weeping and howling over his unrequited affection.'[118] If he did, it must be admitted that Jenny showed good judgment in rejecting him, as she did also in persistently declining a connection with Hans Christian Andersen. With Mendelssohn, I hasten to explain, there was nothing approximating a love-affair. He was a married man, and neither he nor Jenny had ever experienced the benefit of studying sexual morality under certain of our 'advanced modern thinkers.' Still, his extreme enthusiasm, expressed again and again, does suggest that he may have felt more than friendship for her, though it is quite possible that he himself never realized quite what it was. If we

JENNY LIND WITH HER SON

may trust Barnum — and there is always a question here — Jenny Lind seems to have had a weakness for men of the marble statue variety, for we are told that after Daniel Webster had called on her in Boston, she 'walked up and down the room in great excitement, exclaiming: "Ah! Mr. Barnum, that is a man; I have never before seen such a man!"' [119]

Her first serious love-affair was with Julius Günther, an operatic tenor in Stockholm, to whom she was informally engaged as early as 1844. During her career on the Continent, she seems rather to have drifted away from him. But in 1848, the engagement was definitely renewed and rings were exchanged. It seems, however, that Jenny did not love Günther as deeply as she felt she ought to love the man she married. In 1847, she had confessed that she had 'very high thoughts of finding a being, to whom I could utterly and entirely surrender myself.' [120] She did not find him in Günther, and though the details of their parting are not clear, her reluctance to marry an opera singer at the very moment when she herself was trying to break away from the theater seems to have had something to do with it. [121]

The next suitor was an Englishman, Claudius

Harris, a captain in the Indian Army. And oddly enough, as she broke with Günther because he would have kept her in the theater, so she broke with Harris because he insisted on turning her against it. In her own words, he wanted her 'to think the theatre a temple of Satan, and all the actors priests of the Devil.' She was 'not only to abandon her profession, but to be ashamed of it,' and 'to go down to Bath, among people who care for nothing but clergymen and sermons, as a sort of convert or penitent.' The man was not satisfied with her bare word: he wanted her solemn promise that she would never play again actually written into the marriage settlement. Well! She, Jenny Lind, who had all her life been honored as the Christian singer — she was not going to do a thing like that! It showed how small this silly little man's understanding of her was that he should ever have expected that she would.

There was an added difficulty, moreover, in the fact that, though Captain Harris regarded the theater as 'a temple of Satan,' he had not the slightest objection to coming into possession of money that had been earned there. Indeed, while the question of marriage was being discussed, both he and his mother — a formidable lady who looms up somewhat ogreishly in the background of the story — sternly informed Jenny Lind that it would be 'unscriptural' if she were to attempt to control her own fortune after marriage. Now, Jenny Lind liked to give, but she also liked to be a free agent, and she saw no particular reason, either in the Scriptures or out of them, why Captain Claudius Harris should control a fortune not one penny of which he had ever earned.

Finally, after many misgivings, she decided that in spite of everything she would go through with it. Captain Harris threatened her with eternal damnation if she broke her engagement, and she seems to have felt that he was an authority on the subject. But, alas! the anticlimax: 'when in the joy of reconciliation she was singing to him, she turned round and saw that he had gone to sleep.' ¹²² Now, Jenny Lind could marry a man who would not have her without her fortune; she could even marry a man who threatened her with eternal damnation. But to ask her to marry a man who could not keep awake while she was singing — no! that was too much to expect. The whole thing is as lovely a comedy of errors as you are likely to find in a long summer's day, and of all those who have dragged themselves into history on the skirts of the great, none ever succeeded more gloriously in making a complete fool of himself than did Captain Claudius Harris.

And then, finally, there was Otto Goldschmidt. She seems to have met him first in Germany, where he was studying music at the time of her first great Continental triumphs. In England, he played accompaniments for her. When Benedict fell ill in America, she sent for him. He came at once, and though he was eight years younger than she was, they soon fell in love. He was one of the few who could satisfy her as an accompanist, a matter about which she was extremely particular. 'Herr Goldschmidt is our accompanist, and whether he accompanies me or I accompany myself, it is absolutely the same thing.' [123] Unquestionably Goldschmidt knew his business, but there was no glamour about him and audiences often found him dull. All Jenny Lind's native stubbornness came out in response to the challenge. Instead of going back-stage to rest during his piano numbers, she stationed herself on the platform and listened to him attentively, and once, when the audience had been exceptionally rude to him, she delivered a cutting rebuke by

138

JENNY LIND AND HER HUSBAND

meeting him as he was leaving the stage and warmly shaking his hand.[124]   Goldschmidt was a Jew by birth, but in 1851 he was converted to the Christian faith, Jenny Lind standing sponsor for him at his baptism.[125]   On February 5, 1852, they were married in Boston and Edward Everett witnessed the ceremony.[126]   Thereafter her concert billing read: 'Madame Otto Goldschmidt (late Mlle. Jenny Lind).' It is evident that in a good many things Goldschmidt was inevitably subordinated to her. Even Milton realized that such things do happen when the wife is a good deal bigger than her husband! But, in theory at least, she was always firmly of the conviction that the man is the head of the house. In private life she called herself 'Madame Lind-Goldschmidt' and was, says her daughter, 'mortally offended if addressed otherwise.' [127] When her English neighbors referred to Goldschmidt jocosely as 'the Prince Consort of Song,' she was very angry, and found her own way of expressing her displeasure at the intimation 'that her husband should be put second, instead of first, in their home.' [128]

Otto Goldschmidt has, first and last, served as the target of a good deal of unmerited abuse. For some mysterious reason, the world has always regarded it as rather disgraceful for a man to marry a woman who is more famous than he is himself, and Goldschmidt's entire lack of humor,[129] combined with the fact that his virtues were all of the substantial, and none of the scintillating, variety, has always made him an easy subject for attack. But whatever others may have thought, Jenny Lind herself seems to have been always more than satisfied with her bargain, and that, I suppose, is the principal thing. To be sure, the gossips got busy before the honeymoon was over, but there is nothing at all surprising about that. The talk began to reach Jenny while they were still living at Northampton, Massachusetts. 'Why,' she exclaimed, 'I have known him since a boy, and I love him, and am so proud of him, too, for he is a fine composer as well as player.' [130] Much later, in 1871, at a time when the rumors were particularly ugly, she took legal action to silence them.[131] She summed up her impressions of her husband, for the early years at least, in a letter written to Joseph Burke in 1853: 'Mr. Goldschmidt begs me to send you his best compliments, he continues to make justice to my opinion of a true, uninterested friend of mine, he is very kind and faithful to me, bears with

great patience and mildness my many infirmities, and my impulsive nature gets smoothed
by his equal and dignified temper. God bless
and lead him on in the right way, as I have
every reason to love and respect him.'[132]

About her own devotion to him, there can
then be no question whatever: indeed, she
sometimes pushed it beyond the verge of de-
corum. Clara Schumann relates with suitable
indignation that when, in 1853, Jenny was
asked to appear at the Düsseldorf Festival, 'she
replied at once that she would sing gratis if they
would let her husband conduct the Festival.' [133]
The offer was accepted.

I think we must conclude Jenny Lind to have
been happy in her married life. The possibility,
that when she praised her husband to the world,
she was deliberately creating a smoke screen, is
hardly worth considering. Her ideas concerning marriage were extremely conventional —
granted. But she was a very independent
woman, nevertheless, and she had a mind of her
own. Otto Goldschmidt survived his wife for
twenty years, and gave every sign of the sincer-
est devotion to her memory. Mr. Westervelt
tells a very interesting and pathetic story about
what a London shopkeeper said to him one

day when he was buying a Jenny Lind memento.

'... "Some years ago," he proffered, "an odd old chap used to keep popping in here; looked kind of down at the heel; always asked for medals and portraits of Jenny Lind."

'"What was his name?" I queried, scenting a rival collector.

'"I don't remember; guess he's dead by now" — then to his partner: "Jim, what was the name of that queer cove who used to bother us about Jenny Lind stuff? — Heh? Oh, yes" — then to me: "It was Otto Goldschmidt."' [134]

IX

No consideration of Jenny Lind could be complete without some reference to her charities. Nothing about her was more characteristic than her conviction that the money she made did not belong to herself alone, but must be invested where it would do most good for God and for mankind.

It might be supposed that a woman who so thoroughly appreciated the value of money and its importance would have a good business sense, but this does not seem to have been the case. To be sure, Barnum's own account of the

increase in the honorarium for the American
concerts beyond and above what had been
provided for in the contract, as proceeding
entirely from his own generosity, is contra-
dicted by Maunsell B. Field, the lawyer in the
case, who insists that not once but many times
Jenny demanded that the contract be altered,
always to her own advantage, and that every
time Barnum yielded at once with remarkably
good grace and every show of willingness.[135]
And Barnum himself says that before he got
through with her, her 'advisers' harassed him
so much that he was very willing to come to
the end of their agreement.[136] But that does not
mean that she understood the science of money,
or that if she had been left to her own devices
she would have made very much of it. She had
already shown her innocence in this regard in
connection with the Bunn negotiations in England, and her principal contributions to her
American manager consisted of a series of com-
plaints that he was charging too much money
for tickets. After she had left Barnum's management, she remarked to him one day that it was
very annoying to give concerts on her own,
since everybody cheated her.[137]

Nevertheless, she wanted a lot of money — to

give away, and probably no other singer ever gave away so much of it as she did. She was almost as much interested in charity as she was in singing, and her very contract provided that, after she had sung twice for Barnum in any city, she should be free to sing again for charity if she chose. In Sweden, she never sang a note for her own profit after she had become famous. Of the ten thousand dollars which was her share of the proceeds of the first New York concert, she herself never saw a penny. It was divided among the charitable institutions of the city, the apportionment being determined by Barnum and the Mayor of New York. As a matter of fact, none of the money Jenny Lind earned in America was for herself. She kept it in a separate fund, and only twice in her life did she dip into it. At her death, it was devoted to benevolent purposes.[138]

But statistics cannot tell the whole story. In many cases she herself selected the object of her benevolence and personally bestowed the gift. Of course — and here again she suggests Dickens — she was the object of shameful persecution from genteel beggars of every sort. When thoroughly aroused, she could assert herself quite proudly, and Maunsell B. Field says that

CORRESPONDENCE BETWEEN BARNUM
AND JENNY LIND, OCTOBER, 1850

the way she once ordered out an insolent Swedish beggar 'would have done credit to Rachel or Ristori.' [139] But it is clear that she was long-suffering enough, and in many cases she was overwhelmed with reproaches instead of thanks as is the way of the world in such cases. But on the whole, she always preferred to run the risk of being cheated rather than to withhold help where help was really deserved.

There is the pretty story of her secretary coming in one day to tell her, amid much laughter, that he had stood next to a poor girl in the lobby who had paid three dollars for a ticket with the remark, 'There goes a week's wages, but I must hear Jenny Lind.' Forthwith he was hurried out to search the audience for that girl and present her with twenty dollars with Jenny Lind's compliments. [140] And there was the student in a German university who wrote her how desperately anxious he was to hear her, begged her to send him a ticket, and promised to pay her for it as soon as he received his next allowance. Jenny immediately sent two complimentary tickets, and, remembering their location, thoughtfully rewarded the boy's devotion with a smile from the stage. [141] Best of all, there is the story of the poor woman in the country.

Wandering along a lonely road, one day, Jenny
Lind stopped at a little cottage and asked for a
drink of water. The woman was friendly, and
the singer sat down to rest for a while and chat.
The story she heard was one of poverty and
misfortune. Jenny Lind's name came into the
conversation somehow, and the woman asked
her guest if she had ever heard her. 'Yes,' she
replied, 'I, too, am a singer, and if you like, I
will sing you one of Jenny's songs.' When she
had finished, she added, 'Now you, too, may
say that you have heard Jenny sing,' and
pressing a five-pound note into her astonished
companion's hand, she left the cottage immediately, without waiting to be thanked.[142] Is it
any wonder that Jenny Lind was loved? It was
good to do these things, better than being a
great singer, and it warms the heart to read of
them today in yellowing and crumbling books.

But there are those who insist that Jenny
Lind has been praised quite long enough for
her charities; that they were all part of a well-
planned publicity campaign, a good invest-
ment, deliberately calculated to pay large
dividends. And then, because the woman herself had a horror of being thanked, a pronounced dislike for receiving testimonials in re-

146

turn for her charities, they go on to tell us that
she gave, not because she wanted to, but because she felt she had to — God was watching,
and she was buying off the vengeance which
might otherwise fall upon her as a punishment
for her success, her selfishness in keeping the
rewards thereof to herself. In other words,
Jenny Lind was insincere in her charities both
because she did let her left hand know what
her right was doing—and because she didn't.
There is no merit attaching to one who plays
the grand lady as she did and distributes bene-
fits to her inferiors. She is simply wallowing in
sentimental benevolence. In this enlightened
age, there are no inferiors. Charity, in short, is
an anodyne administered by those who are interested in maintaining the *status quo*.

It is perfectly true that Jenny Lind felt it was
her duty to be charitable. 'I feel bound, in one
way or another, to prove in a practical way my
thankfulness to God, who has given me so much
prosperity.' [143] It is perfectly true also that she
could not have slept at night if she had hoarded
her wealth instead of sharing it with others who
needed it more than she. But he who pretends
that therefore she gave grudgingly and cal-
culatingly is simply talking nonsense and mak-

147

ing her over into his own image. Undoubtedly
when the perfect society comes, charity will no
longer be necessary, but to make that a reason
for dispensing with it now would be a curious
sort of benevolence. 'That 'scuse,' as Portia
would say, 'serves many men to save their gifts.'
Jenny Lind might not take high rank as a
political economist, but she knew she was not
living in a perfect society, she did have common-
sense, and, best of all, she had a big heart.

Of the various managers who came in contact with Jenny Lind during her career, perhaps
P. T. Barnum understood her as well as any.
They annoyed each other considerably on more
than one occasion, for they were about as unlike as two persons could well be. In after years,
Jenny Lind once complained of Barnum that he
'exhibited me just as he did the big giant or any
other of his monstrosities.' [144] And he was not
blind to her shortcomings either. 'Like most
persons of strong talent,' he wrote in his autobiography, 'she had a strong will which, at
times, she found ungovernable; but if she was
ever betrayed into a display of ill-temper she
was sure to apologize and express her regret
afterwards. Le Grand Smith, who was quite
intimate with her, and who was my right-hand

man during the entire Lind engagement, used sometimes to say to me: "Well, Mr. Barnum, you have managed wonderfully in always keeping Jenny's 'angel' side outside with the public." ' But Barnum appreciated her good qualities also, declaring as he looked back, after many years, on the greatest enterprise of his career, 'I think now that her natural impulses were more simple, childlike, pure, and generous than those of almost any other person I ever met.' [145]

II

THE ARTIST, THE WOMAN AND GOD

IV
THE ARTIST, THE WOMAN, AND GOD

I want to be near trees; and water; and a cathedral.

JENNY LIND, 1849

She passed *through* life. That is what she made one feel: she was on her way somewhere else: it was a movement across a scene — her life. On she passed: often in perplexity and surprise at what she found here.

HENRY SCOTT HOLLAND

A feeling of uplifted life spread over the metropolis. She melted the souls of thousands, and purged the craft of money getting. We came away from her as from a higher realm.

EDGAR LEE MASTERS, *Children of the Market Place*

CHAPTER IV

The Artist, The Woman, and God

I

BUT there was one absorbing interest, one abiding, all-embracing passion, one goal for life and life's longings that stirred Jenny Lind always much more deeply and thrilled her more profoundly than all the varied wonders of the great world of music and art; that was, indeed, finally in her own career to fuse with her art itself and color it and crown it and give it any such significance as it might come to possess. That passion, that goal was God. 'I have always put God first,' she told her biographer, and she quoted with approval Janotha's saying, 'What is this "world," of which people speak? I do not know what "the world" is. I play for Jesus Christ.' [1] When Jenny was four years old, her religious impulses were first awakened by her maternal grandmother. Not until much later did she realize that her religion was vitally and intimately connected with the musical aspirations that so early engrossed her: it is said to have been the composer Adolf Lindblad who taught her, as she was later to teach Hans Andersen, that the artistic life is itself a conse-

153

cration of the artist and all his powers to God. Thenceforth the core of her being was sound and whole.

Where the first impulse came from is, however, a question of no particular importance, for the spirit of intense moral earnestness so characteristic of the period took possession of Jenny Lind from her earliest childhood, and her temperament and environment being as they were, it was inevitable that this spirit should express itself through religious channels. There was even a bit of ascetic austerity in her nature, for all her sensitiveness to beauty. When she was a child, her mother dressed her in gay colors, but the little girl so hated them that, as soon as she was out of the sight of home, she would pull the bright feathers from her bonnet and hide them.[2] There was something in her that could find no satisfaction in earthly triumphs, no matter how splendid they might be. 'Mother, mother,' she writes Madame Birch-Pfeiffer, at the height of her career, 'I do not belong to this world; my heart will not stay in its narrow prison!'[3] She saw the world always in the light of the spirit. 'Here are thousands of beautiful things certainly, and life in Europe is rich and full of Art and Poetry, but except England

154

there is here everywhere great *infidelity*, great
want of moral activity. People here mostly misunderstand life's claim, object, and end — and
this makes me to feel a stranger. Surrounded
though I am by Kind People, I feel already as
if I was to spend my whole life in Germany, my
soul and my faculties would remain undevel-
oped for want of such examples as I have seen in
England and in America, and yet how many
good qualities do the Germans possess, but —
the *Pride* makes them blind — and Pride is our
greatest and most dangerous *foe*.' [4] And her
own Sweden, much as she loved it, was meas-
ured by a standard no less austere, the standard
she had found in what she never forgot was her
real country — the Kingdom of Heaven. 'There
is here, I confess,' she wrote after her return
from the Continent, 'such frivolousness in everything, that I am sad.... I sometimes doubt
whether I can find joy and happiness here....
The last three years have given me a great deal
clearer insight. Do not imagine that they do
not treat me well; on the contrary: I have nothing at all to complain of, myself: only, it does
pain me that our nation should, through French
influence, have lost so much of its true self.' [5]

Tracing the development of Jenny Lind's

religious conceptions may not seem, on first consideration, in all respects a rewarding task. Hers was not particularly an artist's faith, nor is there much of mystic charm or splendor suggested in connection with it. She lived and died within the comparatively narrow limits of an extremely conventional Lutheran creed, and Lutheranism is the prose, not the poetry, of religion. One may well feel that there is too much emphasis on the negative, the formal, the decorous, too much deliberate narrowing of experience: purely external matters — like the question of traveling on the Sabbath — are granted much more importance than they actually possess. It is said, too, that she was extremely superstitious, would not pass under a ladder if she could avoid it, and if she did, through some inadvertence, always said a little prayer and went on her way rejoicing that all evil had been averted. She is often preoccupied with the 'moral,' in the narrower, fussier sense. Of course, she was not entirely consistent in such matters, any more than the rest of us are, and sometimes the charm of a particular personality would completely conquer her prejudices, or her principles as the case might be. So she accepted Chopin into her circle of

friends, called him a 'good' man, and made
vain excuses for his intrigue with George Sand.[6]
But on the whole the thought of 'duty' intrudes
somewhat too frequently, and it may be partly
as a result of this that one feels that the thrilling
notes of love and passion do not vibrate quite
often enough.

To be sure, there are not many of even the
genuine sons and daughters of God — and I
would not for a moment deny Jenny Lind the
right to inclusion in that company — who can
travel the whole length of the road with Saint
Francis of Assisi, serving God whole-heartedly
with body and soul, shrinking from no sacrifice,
yet finding it all 'sweet and easy.' Yet the
Christian spirit at its best tends inevitably in
that direction, and to some of us it seems that
John Milton's determination to live his life as
ever in his great Taskmaster's eye is just about
as far from the spirit of Christ as it is possible
for a good man to travel. There are many con-
noisseurs of the spirit who have stopped a long
way this side of Saint Francis who have yet —
it seems to me — grasped much more clearly
and definitely than did Jenny Lind the Fourth
Gospel's masterly distinction between the 'servants' and the 'friends' of Christ.

157

At least, it is evident that many of those with whom Jenny Lind came into contact, either socially or through business, felt the rather repelling austerity of her religion: place the fault where you will, what she gave them was a suggestion of oppressive, rather than of winning, religious earnestness. Herr Ödman and others among the Stockholm singers were troubled by this. Joachim speaks of her 'thoughtless, superficial piety — she often invokes God when talking of the most ungodly things, such as money and fame.' 7 And when Maude Valérie White met her as 'an old lady in rather a severe poke bonnet,' she listened impatiently to Jenny's pietistic harangue. 'While she was speaking to me I felt as if I were being birched! I longed to say something frivolous, something positively outrageous.' 8

It may be, of course, that Jenny Lind did not agree with Joachim that money and fame were 'ungodly.' Certainly she never made an ungodly use of either. And it is clear enough that her piety was really neither 'thoughtless' nor 'superficial.' The point is rather that alongside of genuine religious feeling and sensitiveness she had that abominable Victorian pietism that always so strongly irritated Dickens, as he

158

saw it in many of his contemporaries, and that he castigated mercilessly in novel after novel. It is because of this element of conventionality in her that Jenny Lind's expressions of her longing for union with God are less moving than, for example, those of Katherine Mansfield, who was inferior to her in many ways, and infinitely less so than the passionate, pitiful, rebellious outcries of Marie Bashkirtseff.

One hears this note of cold austerity in connection with Jenny Lind's religion on more than one occasion. When Clara Schumann was robbed, she wrote her a letter of condolence in which she said, 'There must certainly be a hell in store for the wicked, wicked men.' Then, catching herself, she adds, 'At least they must be far from God — and that is hell enough.' [9] Her prejudice against the French has been frequently referred to. When Ruskin met her, in 1849, she told him that this people 'seemed to be a nation shut out from the common portion of God's blessing upon men, and deservedly so.' Ruskin tried his best to put in a good word for them, saying 'that the peasantry were not altogether spoiled, that they only wanted an honest government and true religion. "You have said All in that last word," she replied.' [10] At the

time of the Franco-Prussian War she sponsored
a fund for the relief of wounded soldiers.
Arthur Coleridge contributed to it, stipulating
that he wanted half of his money given to
the French. Jenny, who was much less im-
partial, was furious. 'How can you help those
devils?' she asked him.[11] It would perhaps be
somewhat unkind to refer at this point to Swift's
cutting rebuke of those who have just enough
religion to make them hate and not enough to
make them love one another, but I am by no
means sure that it would be unjust.

The dislike of Catholicism comes out again,
much more amusingly, in Liza Lehmann's story
of what happened one day when she and her
mother were having tea with Jenny. A little
Italian boy brought in the muffins, 'and when
he had left the room, she turned to us and in a
tense voice said, "You see that boy? I am trying to conquer myself — to *bear* with him — but
— *he is a Roman Catholic!*"' [12] And she could be
something of a spiritual snob even when there
was no creedal prejudice involved. When her
boat passed Blackwell's Island *en route* from New
York to Boston, the prisoners were gathered on
the shore that they might wave greetings to her
as she passed. She was pleased at first, but

when she was told that these men were con-
victs, she refused to acknowledge their salute
and hurried, as quickly as possible, to the other
side of the boat.[13]

But certainly that is not the whole story, and
it would be absurd and unjust to leave it there.
To Jenny Lind herself it seemed, as she grew
older, that she was gaining in grace and in
strength, that in return for her devotion the
good God was giving more and more of himself to her. 'Ah! much, very much,' she wrote
in 1850, 'must one live through, before one
learns to fasten on the Life, the Higher Life.'
Of the Bible she writes, 'I drink therein rest,
self-knowledge, hope, faith, love, carefulness, and
the fear of God; so that I look at life and the
world in quite another fashion to what I did
before.' [14] In religion she found finally an excitement, a stimulus that made everything the
theater had given her seem hollow and artificial. Late in life she wrote that all stage tears
were sham tears, and quoted the words written
on the margin of her Bible: 'my newly-found
Lord, who first taught me to shed the genuine
tears.' [15]

And religion itself did not always bring her
peace. In her twenties she had been much

troubled with spiritual doubts and difficulties.[16] These passed away in later life, but now and then they would return to plague her. Not long before her death, Henry Scott Holland found her one day pondering over the old questions — the great unanswered problem from the Book of Job to 'The Bridge of San Luis Rey' — ' "Why is evil so strong? Why does wickedness increase? Why is there pain, and misery, and earthquake, and famine, and war? Why does the good which one sets oneself to do, fail? Why do the best efforts win no fruit?" The old desperate enquiries! They stirred her to the very depths. The faith which she firmly grasped for her own salvation, did not seem to spread out as an illuminative interpretation of the world around her.'[17]

Sometimes the light would seem to break through from another world. When she looked on the dead face of her friend, Mrs. Nassau Senior, she caught an impressive glimpse of it. 'It was not her *own* look that was in her face. It was the look of another, that had passed into hers. It was the shadow of Christ that had come upon her. She had seen Christ. And I put down my candle, and I said, "Let me see this thing. Let me stop here always. Let me sit and look.

Where are my children? Let them come and
see. Here is a woman who has seen Christ."' [18]
For herself she was sure that she, too, would one
day look upon His face. 'I feel very strongly the
beginning of the end, and think it a blessing to
look forward to eternal rest. What is the whole
miserable earthly life worth in comparison to one
single glance at the sinless, holy Saviour?' [19]

The faults of Jenny Lind's religion — her
narrowness and her occasional lack of sensitiveness — belonged to her age and to her surroundings: she herself was not directly responsible for them. There can be no question of her
absolute loyalty to the Highest Good she knew.
And we can hardly judge human beings by
reference to the correctness of their ideals: the
only true criterion is their faithfulness to such
ideals as they have. Jenny Lind's God may
have been a caricature of the True God, but so
is mine — and yours. So is every man's.
Religion itself, as Josiah Royce was fond of
insisting, is essentially loyalty. Judged by this
test, Jenny Lind must be rated high.

II

But the great problem in Jenny Lind is the
curious interworking of her religion and her

career. She herself was of the opinion that without religion she could not have had any career that was worth having. 'She told Catherine,' writes Mrs. Stanley, the wife of the Bishop of Norwich, 'that, every morning, when she got up, she felt that her voice was a gift from God, and that, perhaps, that very day might be the last of it.' [20] Others, of course, have felt this. Only a few years ago, Miss Geraldine Farrar, so different from Jenny Lind in so many ways, wrote, on the first page of her autobiography: 'I believe that a benevolent Fate has had watch over me.... This God-sent gift of song was bestowed upon me for some purpose, I know not what. It may fail me, to-morrow, to-night; at any moment something may mar the delicate instrument, and then all the perseverance, pluck, study, and luck in the world will not restore it to me.' [21] And it is said of one of the most famous sopranos of the Metropolitan Opera House that she will not step onto the stage without first making the sign of the cross.

What is highly unusual in Jenny Lind is the steadiness, the consistency with which she regarded each phase of her career as under divine direction. She was led to Paris, to Garcia. She

was led to London: '... things have really so
shaped themselves, that I can see clearly that
God Himself has so ordained it — and, against
one's destiny, one can do nothing.' [22] When
she crossed the ocean to America, again God's
Hand pointed the way: 'I have for a long time
had a most eager wish to earn, somewhere, a
great deal of money, so as to endow a school,
for poor, lost children, in my native country.
And the invitation to America came as a direct
answer, so that I go there in this confidence;
and I pray to God in Heaven, out of a full
heart, that he will guide me thither as ever before, with his gentle hand; and will graciously
forgive me my sins, and my infirmities. But
since I have no less an aim before me than to
help in widening God's Kingdom, the little-
nesses of life vanish in face of this.' [23] It was
from this vantage-point that she justified the
'heavenly — yes, heavenly career' that was hers.
'If you knew what a sensation of the nearness
of a higher power one instinctively feels, when
one is permitted to contribute to the good of
mankind, as I have done, and still do! Believe
me, it is a great gift of God's mercy.' [24]

I have spoken elsewhere of the more fanatical
Jenny Lind adorers who, not satisfied to ad-

mire a woman, insist on worshiping a saint, who, specifically, refuse to admit in her the existence of any vestige of that personal ambition and honest self-seeking that seems to be incidental to being human and to being an artist. The question arises again in this distinctively religious connection. Jenny Lind herself prayed that the influence of what she gave to mankind might never die. 'My unceasing prayer is, that what I gave my fellows may continue to live on through eternity, and that the Giver of the gift, and not the creature to whom He lent it, may be praised and acknowledged.' [25] It may be that her prayer will be answered. At least her influence has long outlasted that of any other singer of her time, and Madame Frieda Hempel, who has given much time and thought to the subject in recent years, once told Mr. Westervelt that she felt Jenny Lind was not dead. But is she not, in this very utterance, profoundly conscious of self? Here is the problem that has so curiously intrigued Gamaliel Bradford in his observation of this type of personality: in his portrait of Frances Willard,[26] in the full-length study of D. L. Moody,[27] and, above all, in that profound and subtle probing of our efforts at once to assert our individuality and to escape from it, 'Life and I.' [28] Oh, I know that it is on the Not-I that the 'official' emphasis in every such case is placed. Here it is that Jenny Lind places it: it is 'the Giver of the gift, and not the creature to whom He lent it,' that she wishes to have remembered. But at the same time, it is *her* gift that she is concerned about: she does not make Henrietta Nissen's the subject of her prayers! How could Moody or Miss Willard possibly have made a greater name for themselves in a career of self-aggrandizement than they did in the service of God? How, for that matter, could Saint Francis of Assisi, who probably came as close to complete self-abnegation as any man that Western civilization has yet produced? It is the old paradox of losing one's life for the sake of finding it. Or, at least, of losing it with that result. And just as it is possible to argue plausibly that the thoroughgoing ascetic is at least as much preoccupied with sex as the libertine, so it sometimes seems as if those who lose their lives in God, or who think they do, often secure a fuller and more magnificent expression of their own ego than any others among the sons of men.

But there have always been those who have

urged that it was Jenny Lind's religion that put
an end to her career; that if it had not been for
religion she would have continued longer in the
theater and won an even prouder place in the
history of music. Even so devoted an admirer
as Hans Christian Andersen was firmly of this
opinion. 'She has left the stage,' he wrote; 'that
is a wrong done her spirit; it is to give up her
mission, the mission that God chose for her.' [29]
And Mr. Werner remarks that 'she was held
back from supreme artistic triumph in this
world that she might enjoy comfort in the next,
and it is to be hoped that her spiritual promises
to herself have been fulfilled.' [30]

The answer depends somewhat upon what
one's conception of a great career is. Jenny
Lind had limitations of health and of temperament that would probably have taken her into
retirement at a fairly early age even if religion
had not been there profoundly to reënforce
them. For the theater is a strange and a complicated thing. It is the eclectic art, the art which
embraces within itself the ministries of all the
others, capable — through its powerful visual
capacity, its tremendous gift of inducing sympathetic realizations — of interpreting and en-
larging the individual's vision of life as nothing

else can do it. But this supreme mistress of the artist soul is not always chaste. There are too many rhinestones on her gown and her cheeks are heavily rouged. She is Cleopatra, not Desdemona:

> Age cannot wither her, nor custom stale
> Her infinite variety.

It is frequently taken for granted that Jenny Lind left the stage because, under the influence of her English friends, the Stanleys and others, she had gone over to the extreme Puritanical position that the theater is the abode of wickedness. This is somewhat misleading. To be sure, Charlotte Bournonville relates how, in 1854, Jenny told her father that she now considered it a sin to appear in a theater. How can that be? asked Bournonville. When you sang in the theater, you made it a church. You brought a spiritual message to those who could not be reached in any other way. Now that you confine yourself to churches, people go to divine service, not to worship God, but to hear your voice. Which is better, to bring the church into the theater or to bring the theater into the church? Goldschmidt agreed entirely with Bournonville's reasoning, but Jenny became angry and dismissed the matter by saying that since the Archbishop of Canterbury had said it was a sin to sing in a theater, the matter was no longer open for discussion.[31] But this certainly was not her permanent mood. She invested much interest and energy long years after her retirement in training others for a theatrical career, and she was hardly the woman to gather recruits for the House of Belial. Moreover, her letters show clearly that she had determined fully to retire long before she ever met the Stanleys. What she did feel, quite steadily, was not that the theater was evil, but that she herself could not achieve what her spirit craved in the distracting surroundings of back-stage life. For that she needed something different altogether: 'trees; and water; and a cathedral.' So she gave it all up, and it must have cost her something to do it.

Just what is an artist, anyway, and what is his talent? And how far is the development of the artist as artist dependent on and conditioned by his development as a human being? The question arises again, most poignantly, in the case of Katherine Mansfield, who came, some time before the end of her life, to the feeling that she had gone as far as she could go in her art with-

out a spiritual regeneration of herself, who
therefore stopped writing to stake everything
upon that rebuilding of life, and who, at the
very end, magnificently won the victory, though
she did not live long enough afterwards to share
it with the world in the 'different' stories she
was going to write. Much happier has been the
experience of Miss Geraldine Farrar. 'In the
back of my head, through all my operatic
years,' she writes, 'especially during the latter
half of them, I was always conscious of the
necessity for definite progress, and by that statement I mean the progress that would develop
me as a woman as well as an artist.' When the
time came to leave the opera, '... I realized
that I must learn something more of life. I
knew that it was of supreme importance that I
learn to know what sort of woman I was and
that I was to be.' Then, after the trying period
of readjustment, came the return as a Lieder
singer. 'I sang as I have never spiritually sung
before, because in this singing I had chosen fine
singing, splendid development, with no ulterior
appeal to the banal. A public excessively loyal
and kind to me always grasped this effort of
mine, and, to my intense gratitude, accepted it.
I am more grateful, as a woman, than I can

say.' [32] Jenny Lind would have understood that experience, different as it was from her own. We often think of an artist's talent as if it were something outside of the artist himself. We even debate, fatuously, whether the source of So-and-So's appeal is her art or her personality! But for Jenny Lind her art was significant only as an expression of her personality, and whatever hindered her soul-development could not be regarded as anything else than a handicap in her art.

One asks one's self whether the baser, coarser side of the theater ever tempted her. The answer must be yes and no. Debauchery and promiscuity could hold no charm for the austerity of that spirit. But there are other things in theatrical life, more alluring than debauchery and promiscuity. There are glitter and tinsel and vanity, the temptation to take the show for the reality, to enter so readily into the joys and sorrows of others that one has no energy left to build a set of honest emotional reactions for one's self. And these things I think there is no doubt that Jenny Lind felt. Her authorized biographers, who knew her well, assure us that she had the artistic temperament with all its temptations and difficulties, and that it cost her a hard struggle to bring it within bounds.[33] That she could not achieve it, to her own satisfaction at least, as long as she remained in the theater, is perhaps not wholly without significance: there are others who have achieved it under just these circumstances. On January 8, 1845, she wrote a letter filled with rejoicing over her triumph in 'Das Feldlager in Schlesien': 'Sontag herself had not so brilliant a triumph.' 'I almost think I achieved a greater triumph than in *Norma*.' She goes on to tell of a happy evening spent in visiting Goethe's Bettina. 'We did not return till after twelve!' Finally, she adds significantly: 'Nowadays the world is influencing me very considerably.' [34] It has its comic side — this dreadful dissipation of visiting Goethe's Bettina and staying out until after twelve! Nevertheless, she seems to have felt that there were possibilities in that direction. And far more significant is the priceless story of the friend who found her, once in England, on the seashore, with an open Bible in her lap, looking out into the sunset. 'Oh, Madame Goldschmidt, how was it that you ever came to abandon the stage, at the very height of your success?' And she replied quietly, 'When, every day, it made me think less of *this*' (laying her finger on the Bible) 'and nothing at all of *that*' (pointing to the sunset), 'what else could I do?' ³⁵

III

So it seems to me that Jenny Lind's religion, despite all my reservations concerning it, gave to her art far more than it took away. It is quite possible that without it she would have sung more rôles and sung longer, but she could never have made the peculiar impression that is associated with her name. As I have said before, if the artist is only an artist he is nothing, and it was not on the technical basis alone that Jenny was ever judged or on which she would have wished to be judged.

Above everything else, she gave her audiences the impression that they were seeing and listening to an exceptionally pure, an exceptionally noble woman, and it was for this as much as for anything that she was loved. Yes, as much as for her talent, for if her purity could not have made its impression without her talent, neither could her talent have done it without her purity. And the public was not deceived: she was an exceptionally pure, an exceptionally noble woman. With all her foibles and all her shortcom-

174

ings, there is no doubt whatever about that. She stood before the world as an artist, a priestess of beauty, but she sensed, as the Greeks did, the underlying harmony of the beautiful and the good. In her mind they could not be separated from each other. Once she spoke to J. A. Symonds of 'the sorrow of sin which destroys beauty. We who have an ideal see that, and cannot bear the discord.' [36]

Sympathetic critics sensed this spiritual exaltation of Jenny Lind's art from the beginning of her career. 'One sentiment...' wrote a German critic in 1846, 'pervades all her Art-pictures — the spirit of holiness....' [37] Meyerbeer speaks of 'those indelible graces which modesty and candour and innocence give only to their favored ones.' [38] And Hans Christian Andersen testified, 'Through Jenny Lind I first became sensible of the holiness there is in art; through her I learned that one must forget one's self in the service of the Supreme.' [39]

I have spoken in another connection of her departures from standard conceptions in several of the rôles that she played. Some of these bear testimony, in a very concrete way, to this steadiness of her aspiration after the things of the spirit. Of her Susanna, in 'Figaro,' it was

remarked that she emphasized the womanli-
ness, the loyalty, the purity of the character, be-
neath all the surface frivolities with which other
singers had been content. Of her Amina, in
'La Sonnambula,' one critic wrote: 'She reads
the character differently from all her prede-
cessors — appearing not as a village coquette
... but as a fond, loving girl, faithful to her
lover, and rejecting for his sake the attention of
the stranger count....' [40] Of her Donna Anna,
a German reviewer remarked, 'In one word,
Jenny Lind clothes the part in her own modest
purity — no other conception would be intel-
ligible to her.' [41]

But the best illustration here, because the
most elaborate, is the fundamental change she
made in the psychology of Norma, and that
entirely apart from the question of whether
what she did was legitimate or not. Perhaps
the fundamental difference between her revolutionary interpretation and the more conventional characterization of Giulia Grisi may
best be indicated in the words of Parker Willis:
'Jenny Lind is the betrayed and heart-crushed
woman; Grisi, the jealous mistress, panting for
vengeance for her wrongs.' C. G. Rosenberg's
description may help us to see how the contrast

176

JENNY LIND AS NORMA

worked itself out: 'In the *duo* with *Adalgisa*, or rather in the scene which immediately precedes that *duo*, the grandeur of Grisi is concentred in the moment, when, as if inspired by the spirit of vengeance, she springs forward with the poniard lifted against the lives of her two children. With Jenny Lind it is the pathos of the outcry as she staggers back, unable to consummate her fell design. In Grisi's love for *Pollione*, the senses of the audience are appalled by the intense passion and vehement bitterness of her reproaches. With Jenny it is in the mingled sadness and sorrow of her humble spirit that the observer realizes her passion for the Roman warrior.' [42]

It will be seen, then, that Jenny Lind would have agreed perfectly with Julia Marlowe that 'the dramatic attraction of the woman that stays pure' is the thing that is worth cultivating in the theater. 'A woman of moral depravity,' says Miss Marlowe, 'offers the modern playwright greater scope than a good woman because her life is full of incidents that are dramatic.' But 'it takes a greater artist to make a good woman interesting than to make a base woman sympathetic and thrilling.' [43] What Miss Lind would have thought of the depraved

women of many of our popular modern plays
— our Madeleine Carys and our Mary Dugans
and our Nina of 'Strange Interlude' — is a
subject which it is better, on the whole, to leave
to the imagination.

To be sure, an artist — or a woman — who
limits herself thus, like Jenny Lind, like Julia
Marlowe, like Lillian Gish — does lose something as well as gain something. There is a
certain robust appeal in the great outcry of
Chaucer's Wife of Bath, compounded as she is
of all the lust and energy of life — (I suspect
Jenny Lind would have found it unutterably
shocking):

> But, Lord Crist! whan that it remembreth me
> Upon my yowthe and on my jolitee,
> It tikleth me aboute myn herte-roote.
> Unto this day it dooth myn herte boote
> That I have had my world, as in my tyme.

Nobody wants the theater to play infinite varia-
tions on the Elsie Dinsmore theme. Nobody
would pretend that it is impossible to build a
great play about an 'erring' woman and treat
the subject in a perfectly legitimate way. I
imagine few persons who were fortunate enough
to witness the magnificent performance of the

late Jeanne Eagels in 'Rain' would deny that
she had widened their experience and deepened
their comprehension of life, and I personally
cannot imagine any one who could suppose
himself or another to have been injured or offended by such a performance and such a play.
Only, as Henry Adams reminds us in his wonderful appreciation of the Virgin of Chartres,
while 'Vulgarity, too, has feeling, and its
expression in art has truth and even pathos,'
still 'we shall have time enough in our lives for
that....' [44] We have time enough, God knows,
in the theater, and enough devotees of the cult.
The few artists who refuse to touch it will always stand, somewhat, in a world apart.

The debate over Jenny Lind's Norma recalls
an incident in the life of Modjeska. One of the
few excursions made by that great actress into
the realm of the *demi-monde* was when she acted
Camille. And on that occasion she seems to
have glorified the character, much as Jenny
Lind was accused of having glorified Norma, so
that by the time she had finished there was much
more of Modjeska than of Camille about her.
'If anything could reconcile judgment to the
drama of "Camille,"' wrote her friend William
Winter, 'which nothing can do, — it would be

179

the embodiment of its heroine, incorrectly and unjustifiably, as she was embodied by Modjeska. She was more like a spirit than a woman; she was the ideal of native purity, lost through passion, but struggling toward the light. I remember a lovely summer night at her home of "Arden," strolling to and fro, with her, through a rose garden, when the actress, knowing my views of that play, began an elaborate defence of it, based on her performance of its chief part. Very interesting her discourse was, — especially when, in a moment of charming candour, after reviewing the expedients and details of her personation, she remarked, "Of course, it isn't *Camille* at all, but then —," and, perceiving the superficiality of further comment, ceased to speak.' [45]

I wonder if Modjeska should have ceased to speak at quite that point. Just how far is an actress bound to be 'faithful' to the dramatist whose character she represents? It is idle to answer 'Completely,' for complete faithfulness exists only in theory. Many years ago, Miss Maxine Elliott remarked that a good actress is more important than any play, and there is a sense in which the words are perfectly true. Many a bad play has been rendered tolerable

by the fact that some great actress had sense
enough to misinterpret it. Many a great character in drama owes quite as much to the first
actor who played the rôle as it owes to the
dramatist who conceived it. In such instances
as Jenny Lind's Norma and Modjeska's Camille,
acting is certainly among the creative arts.

Simply because of Jenny Lind's triumphant
Puritanism, her refusal to be actuated by base
motives in life or to represent them on the stage,
some observers found her cold. One feels that
a good many of the gentlemen who are now engaged in the gentle art of moulding and edu-
cating our dramatic tastes would have agreed
with them. Thus, one finds even so sane a man
and able a critic as Mr. Barrett H. Clark as-
suring us that he is unable to discriminate in the
theater between a pure emotion and an emotion
that is impure. In Mr. Clark's view, 'a virtuous
young girl is a very lovely thing in her place,'
but 'unless she happens to be your own daughter or you happen to be in love with her, her
place isn't so large or so important.' On the
stage, 'an ordinary prostitute' is much more
interesting. 'Shakespeare knew where to put
the pretty young thing: Ophelia is one of the
stupidest of his characters. He intended that

she should be.' [46] I have always felt Ophelia to
be one of the most misunderstood characters
in the whole range of drama, but, be that as it
may, I submit it is hardly fair to cite her in this
connection. For we may dispose of Ophelia as
we like: we shall still have Juliet, Viola, Portia,
Rosalind, Imogene, Desdemona, and the others.
What are we to do with them? Are they all
'ordinary prostitutes'? Or are they just uninteresting?

This whole matter of 'coldness' in actresses
was conveniently laid to rest in one of William
Winter's comments on Mary Anderson:

'Conventional judgment as to Mary Anderson's acting,' wrote Winter, 'expressed itself in
one statement — "She is cold." There could
not be a greater error. That quality in her acting, — a reflex from her spiritual nature, —
which produced on the conventional mind the
effect of coldness was, in fact, distinction, the attribute of being exceptional. The judgment
that she was cold was a resentful judgment, and
was given in a spirit of detraction. It proceeded
from an order of mind that can never be content with the existence of anything above its own
level.... A woman of the average kind is not
difficult to understand. There is nothing dis-

tinctive about her. She is fond of admiration; rather readily censorious of other women; charitable toward male rakes; and partial to fine attire....

'Women of that sort are not called "cold." The standard is ordinary and it is understood. But when a woman appears on the stage whose life is not ruled by the love of admiration, whose nature is devoid of vanity, who looks with indifference upon adulation, whose head is not turned by renown, whose composure is not disturbed by flattery, whose simplicity is not marred by wealth, who does not go into theatrical hysterics and offer that condition of artificial delirium as the mood of genius in acting, and who above all makes it apparent, in her personality and her achievements, that the soul can be sufficient to itself and can exist without taking on a burden of the fever or dulness of other lives, there is a flutter of vague discontent among the mystified rank and file, and she is called "cold." ' [47]

Though the brief operatic phase will always be remembered as the most brilliant aspect of Jenny Lind's career, she did, of course, spend a much longer period in concert and oratorio singing, and in some respects this was far more characteristic of her. In oratorio especially, she found congenial material. In 1849, she writes: 'I have begun to sing what has long been the wish of my heart — Oratorio. There I can sing the music I love; and the words make me feel a better being.' [48] Here she used no *cadenzas*, no ornamentation of any kind: instead, her singing was marked by a classical severity of style. In his 'Reminiscences,' Lyman Abbott speaks of her interpretation of 'I Know That My Redeemer Liveth': '... it was impossible to doubt the Resurrection while she was singing.... She seemed a celestial witness; to doubt her testimony was to doubt her veracity.' [49] Mr. Werner makes fun of this: '... Jenny Lind surely would not have lied about such a thing as the Resurrection.' And perhaps, he adds, Lyman Abbott, as a young man, may have been somewhat more suspectible to spiritual influences than most of his contemporaries.[50] Very possibly he was. He certainly was in his maturity. But this is hardly *à propos*, for there is nothing singular in his response to Jenny Lind's singing of the 'Redeemer' number. Once, as she finished it, Daniel Webster, surely no particular connoisseur in piety, rose from his seat in the center of the balcony and made her a profound bow. [51] It is said that she always placed the accent on 'know,' thus making the utterance, as it were, a personal confession of faith. [52] Richard Hoffman says that, as she sang it, 'Her rapt expression of face and never-ending volume of voice made her appear like some inspired seraph delivering a divine message.' [53] Appy testifies, 'She sang with such a fervor of religious passion that it caught one up, as it seemed, into the sacred presence.' [54] And George William Curtis declares that 'the lofty fervor of the tone, the rapt exaltation of the woman, with the splendor of the vocalization, made the hearing an event, and left a memory as of a sublime religious function.' [55] This was perhaps her greatest achievement, her supreme expression of herself in art. When she died, the words 'I Know That My Redeemer Liveth' were engraved upon her memorial in Westminster Abbey.

And so my mind goes back to the woman on the seashore. 'When, every day, it made me think less of *this*, and nothing at all of *that*, what else could I do?' The Bible and the sunset! And the world well lost!

There is always a peculiar interest attaching to those who conquer the world and then throw it away. Self-indulgence and vice have generally been the most popular motives for such a relinquishment. Jenny Lind threw it away for God.

THE END

BIBLIOGRAPHY

BIBLIOGRAPHY [1]

Abbott, Lyman: *Reminiscences.* Boston: Houghton Mifflin Company, 1915.

Andersen, Hans Christian: *The Story of My Life.* Author's edition. Boston: Houghton Mifflin Company. [*c*1871.]

Appy, Henri: 'Characteristics of Jenny Lind,' *Century Magazine,* N.S. xxxii (1897), 554–58.

Apthorp, William F. [ed.]: *Hector Berlioz, Selections from his Letters, and Æsthetic, Humorous, and Satirical Writings.* New York: Henry Holt and Company, 1879. (Contains Berlioz's burlesque description of the Jenny Lind excitement in America, pp. 255–61.)

Bancroft, Mr. and Mrs. S. B.: *Mr. and Mrs. Bancroft, On and Off the Stage.* Written by Themselves. Vol. ii. Second edition. London: Richard Bentley and Son, 1888.

Barnum, P. T.: *Struggles and Triumphs: or, The Life of P. T. Barnum.* Written by Himself. Edited, with an Introduction by George S. Bryan. Volume i. New York: Alfred A. Knopf, 1927.

Bayley, F. W. N.: *The Souvenir of the Season. The Wake of Extacy, A Memory of Jenny Lind.* London: Willoughby and Company, 1848. (Bad poetry and worse pictures, 'elegantly' printed in the bad sense of that word.)

---

[1] A complete list of all the literature bearing on Jenny Lind that was consulted in the preparation of this study. Specific indebtedness is indicated in the references hereinafter. Books devoted to other subjects and employed for illustrative purposes do not appear in the bibliography, but adequate information concerning them is given in the notes.

Bibliography

Becher, A. J.: *Jenny Lind, eine Skizze ihres Lebens und ihrer Künstler-Laufbahn bis auf die neuste Zeit*. Second edition. Wien: Jasper, 1847.

Benedict, Sir Julius: 'Jenny Lind,' *Scribner's Monthly*, XXII (1881), 120–32. (Not to be confused with *Scribner's Magazine*.)

Bennett, J. R. Sterndale: *The Life of William Sterndale Bennett*. Cambridge: University Press, 1907.

Benson, A. C., and Viscount Esher: *The Letters of Queen Victoria*. Volume II. New York: Longmans, Green and Company, 1907.

Bickley, Nora [ed.]: *Letters from and to Joseph Joachim*. London: Macmillan and Company, Limited, 1914.

Blaze de Bury, Henri: 'La musique dans le Nord,' *Revue des deux Mondes*, XIV (1852), 521-40.

Bournonville, Charlotte: *Erindringer fra Hjemmet og fra Scenen*. Kjøbenhavn: Gyldendalske Boghandels Forlog, 1903.

Bremont, Anna, Comtesse de: *The World of Music*. New York: Brentano's, 1892.

Broughton, Lord: *Recollections of a Long Life*. With Additional Extracts from His Private Diaries. Edited by his daughter, Lady Dorchester. Volume IV. London: John Murray, 1911.

Brown, Horatio F.: *John Addington Symonds: A Biography*. Compiled from his Papers and Correspondence. Volume I. New York: Charles Scribner's Sons, 1895.

Brown, Horatio F. [ed.]: *Letters and Papers of John Addington Symonds*. London: John Murray, 1923.

Bunn, Alfred: *The Case of Bunn versus Lind* [etc., etc.]. London: W. S. Johnson, 1848.

Bibliography

Butler, William Allen: *Barnum's Parnassus; Being Confidential Disclosures of the Prize Committee on the Jenny Lind Song* [etc.]. New York: D. Appleton and Company, 1850. (As might be inferred from the title, this is a burlesque. Possibly, however, it might be rather less easily inferred that it is an extremely amusing burlesque, one of the few contemporary documents on the Jenny Lind vogue that are still worth reading for their own sakes. The pamphlet was published anonymously, but Butler confesses authorship in his *Retrospect of Forty Years*.)

Butler, William Allen: *A Retrospect of Forty Years, 1825–1865*. New York: Charles Scribner's Sons, 1911.

Carlyle, Alexander [ed.]: *New Letters of Thomas Carlyle*. Volume II. London and New York: John Lane, 1904.

Cartwright, Julia [ed.]: *The Journals of Lady Knightley of Fawsley, 1856–1884*. London: John Murray, 1915.

Cavendish, Lady Frederick: *The Diary of Lady Frederick Cavendish*. Edited by John Bailey. Volume I. London: John Murray, 1927.

Chorley, Henry F.: *Thirty Years' Musical Recollections*. Edited with an Introduction by Ernest Newman. New York: Alfred A. Knopf, 1926.

Clark, John Willis, and Hughes, Thomas McKenny: *The Life and Letters of the Reverend Adam Sedgwick* [etc., etc.]. Volume II. Cambridge: University Press, 1920.

Coleridge, Arthur: *Reminiscences*. London: Constable and Company, Limited, 1921.

Coleridge, Stephen: *Memories*. London: John Lane, 1913.

Congdon, Charles T.: *Reminiscences of a Journalist*. Boston: James R. Osgood and Company, 1880.

Cook, E. T.: *The Life of John Ruskin.* Volume I. London: George Allen and Company, Limited, 1911.

Crosland, Mrs. Newton: *Landmarks of a Literary Life, 1820–1892.* London: Sampson Low, Marston and Company, Limited, 1893.

Curtis, George William: *From the Easy Chair.* New York: Harper and Brothers, 1893.

Dahlgren, Lotten [ed.]: *Grannarna på Kungsängsgatan.* Stockholm: Wahlström and Widstrand, 1904.

Davison, Henry [ed.]: *From Mendelssohn to Wagner. Being the Memoirs of J. W. Davison* [etc.]. London: William Reeves, 1912.

Dietz, Robert Edwin: *1913. A Leaf from the Past. Dietz Then and Now* [etc.]. New York: R. E. Dietz Company [ᶜ1914].

Dorph, Sven: *Jenny Lindiana till hundraårsminnit.* Second edition. Upsala: Lindblad, 1919.

Dorph, Sven: *Jenny Linds triumftåg genom nya världen och övriga levnadsöden.* Second edition. Upsala: Lindblad, 1918.

Edward, H. Sutherland: *The Prima Donna.* Volume II. London: Remington and Company, 1888.

Ellis, William Ashton [ed.]: *Richard to Minna Wagner: Letters to his First Wife.* Volume I. London: H. Grevel and Company, 1909.

Elmblad, Sigrid Agneta Sofia: *Jenny Lind, en livsstudie.* Second edition. Upsala: Lindblad, 1921.

Emerson, Ralph Waldo: *Journals.* With Annotations. Edited by Edward Waldo Emerson and Waldo Emerson Forbes. Volume VIII. Boston: Houghton Mifflin Company, 1912.

Erskine, Mrs. Steuart [ed.]: *Anna Jameson, Letters and Friendships* (1812–1860). London: T. Fisher Unwin, Limited, 1915.

Ferris, George T.: *Great Singers. Malibran to Materna.* Second series. New York: D. Appleton and Company, 1900.

Field, Maunsell B.: *Memories of Many Men and Some Women.* New York: Harper and Brothers, 1874.

Foote, Henry S.: *Casket of Reminiscences.* Washington: Chronicle Publishing Company, 1874.

Foster, C. G.: *Memoir of Jenny Lind* [etc.]. New York: De Witt and Davenport, 1850.

Frothingham, Paul Revere: *Edward Everett, Orator and Statesman.* Boston: Houghton Mifflin Company, 1925.

Ganz, Wilhelm: *Memories of a Musician.* London: John Murray, 1913.

Giacomo Meyerbeer. Jenny Lind. Fragmente aus dem Tagebuch eines alten Musikers [etc.]. Wien: M. Kuppisch, 1847.

Godwin, Parke: *Vala, A Mythological Tale.* New York: George P. Putnam, 1851. (The career of Jenny Lind reviewed in terms of a rather anemic allegory.)

Graves, Charles L.: *The Life and Letters of Sir George Grove, C.B.* London: Macmillan and Company, Limited, 1903.

Greeley, Horace: *Recollections of a Busy Life.* New York: J. B. Ford and Company, 1868.

Greenwood, Grace: *Haps and Mishaps of a Tour in Europe.* London: Richard Bentley and Son, 1854.

Hallé, C. E. and Marie [eds.]: *Life and Letters of Sir*

Charles Hallé [etc.]. London: Smith, Elder, and Company, 1896.

Hamilton, Lord Frederic: *The Days Before Yesterday*. New York: George H. Doran Company, 1920.

Hare, Augustus J. C.: *The Story of My Life*. Volume VI. London: George Allen, 1900.

Haven, Gilbert, and Russell, Thomas: *Life of Father Taylor, The Sailor Preacher*. Boston: Boston Port and Seaman's Aid Society, 1904.

Haweis, H. R.: 'Jenny Lind,' *Contemporary Review*, LIX (1891), 900–11.

Hegermann-Lindencrone, Lillie de: *In the Courts of Memory, 1858–1875*. From Contemporary Letters. New York: Harper and Brothers, 1912.

Higginson, Mary Thacher: *Letters and Journals of Thomas Wentworth Higginson, 1846–1900*. Boston: Houghton Mifflin Company, 1921.

Higginson, Mary Thacher: *Thomas Wentworth Higginson, The Story of his Life*. Boston: Houghton Mifflin Company, 1914.

Hildebrand, W. A., and others: Pamphlet, no title, no date. On cover are the words: 'Jenny Lind Association. New York.' Evidently printed in 1923.

Hoffman, Richard: 'Some Musical Recollections of Fifty Years,' Second article. *Scribner's Magazine*, XLVII (1910), 428–42.

Holland, Henry Scott: 'Jenny Lind,' *Living Age*, CLXXV (1887), 751–57. (An important postscript to the authorized biography.)

Holland, Henry Scott, and Rockstro, W. S.: *Memoir of Madame Jenny Lind-Goldschmidt: Her Early Art-Life and*

Dramatic Career, 1820–1851. From Original Documents, Letters, MS Diaries, &c., Collected by Mr. Otto Goldschmidt. Two volumes. London: John Murray, 1891. (Called on the binding: 'Jenny Lind — The Artist.' The authorized biography of Jenny Lind.)

Holley, Sallie: *A Life for Liberty.* New York: G. P. Putnam's Sons, 1899.

Holmstrom, V. M.: 'Jenny Lind's Singing Method,' *Musical Quarterly,* III (1917), 548–51. (A long and extremely important letter of Jenny Lind.)

Hone, Philip: *The Diary of Philip Hone, 1828–1851.* Edited with an Introduction by Bayard Tuckermann. Volume II. New York: Dodd, Mead and Company, 1889.

Hueffer, Ford Madox: *Ancient Lights and Certain New Reflections. Being the Memories of a Young Man.* London: Chapman and Hall, Limited, 1911.

'Jenny Lind and the Royal College of Music,' *Musical Times,* LXI (1920), 738–39.

Jenny Lind Centennial Celebration Committee: *Press Comments on the Jenny Lind Centennial Celebration, October sixth, 1820–1920.* Two volumes. (Hand-made scrapbooks in the New York Public Library.)

Johnson, Catherine B. [ed.]: *William Bodham Donne and His Friends.* London: Methuen and Company, 1905.

Karasowski, Moritz: *Frederic Chopin. His Life and Letters.* Translated by Emily Hill. Volume II. New York: Charles Scribner's Sons, 1906.

Kellogg, Clara Louise: *Memoirs of an American Prima Donna.* New York: G. P. Putnam's Sons, 1913.

Klein, Herman: *Thirty Years of Musical Life in London, 1870-1900.* New York: The Century Company, 1903.

Kuhe, Wilhelm: *My Musical Recollections*. London: Richard Bentley and Son, 1896.

Lehmann, Liza: *The Life of Liza Lehmann*. By Herself. London: T. Fisher Unwin, Limited, 1919.

Life and Genius of Jenny Lind, The. New York: W. F. Burgess, 1850.

Lillie, Lucy C.: 'Jenny Lind-Goldschmidt,' *Lippincott's Magazine*, XL (1887), 914–26.

Lindiana, An Interesting Narrative of the Life of Jenny Lind. Arundel, Sussex: Mitchell and Son, 1847.

Litzmann, Berthold: *Clara Schumann, An Artist's Life* [etc.]. Translated... by Grace E. Hadow. Two volumes. London: Macmillan and Company, Limited, 1913.

Lives of Good and Great Women. New York: Ward and Drummond, n.d.

Locker-Lampson, Frederick: *My Confidences* [etc.]. London: Smith, Elder and Company, 1896.

Lodge, Henry Cabot: *Early Memories*. New York: Charles Scribner's Sons, 1913.

Longfellow, Samuel: *Life of Henry Wadsworth Longfellow*. Volume II. Boston: Houghton Mifflin Company. [ᶜ1886.]

Lumley, Benjamin: *Reminiscences of the Opera*. London: Hurst and Blackett, 1864.

Mackinlay, M. Sterling: *Garcia the Centenarian and His Times*. Edinburgh: William Blackwood and Sons, 1908.

McNeill, Ronald J.: 'Jenny Lind,' *Century Magazine*, N.S. XXIII (1892), 207–10.

Macpherson, Gerardine: *Memoirs of the Life of Anna Jameson*. Boston: Roberts Brothers, 1878.

Macready, William Charles: *The Diaries of William Charles Macready, 1833–1851*. Edited by William Toynbee. Volume II. New York: G. P. Putnam's Sons, 1912.

Mahomet; or the Unveiled Prophet of Inistan: A Bouquet for Jenny Lind. New York: Published by the Authoress, 1850. (A scurrilous, pietistic, incoherent attack on Barnum as a reincarnation of Mohammed, etc. Jenny Lind's great sin seems to be that she sings in wicked theaters.)

Marsh, Elizabeth LeBaron: 'Jenny Lind in Northampton,' *New England Magazine*, N.S. VI (1892), 393–402. (The principal source of information for Jenny Lind's life in the months immediately following her marriage.)

Masters, Edgar Lee: *Children of the Market Place*. New York: The Macmillan Company, 1922.

Maude, Cyril: *Behind the Scenes with Cyril Maude*. London: John Murray, 1927.

Maude, Mrs. Raymond: *The Life of Jenny Lind*. London: Cassell and Company, Limited, 1926. (Written by Jenny Lind's daughter.)

May, Florence: *The Life of Johannes Brahms*. Volume I. London: Edward Arnold, 1905.

Meighan, Thaddeus W.: *The Jenny Lind Mania in Boston; or, A Sequel to Barnum's Parnassus*. By Asmodeus. Boston, 1850.

Memoir of Jenny Lind. London: John Ollivier, 1847.

Moestin, Marie: *Sångkunstens historie*. Kristiania: Aschehong and Company, 1917.

Moscheles, Mrs. Ignatz: *Life of Moscheles, with Selections from His Diaries and Correspondence*. By His Wife.

Adapted from the Original German by A. D. Coleridge. Volume II. London: Hurst and Blackett, 1873.

Moscheles, Mrs. Ignatz: *Recent Music and Musicians, As Described in the Diaries and Correspondence of Ignatz Moscheles*. Edited by his Wife and adapted from the original German by A. D. Coleridge. New York: Henry Holt and Company, 1889.

Mozley, J. B.: *Letters of the Rev. J. B. Mozley, D.D.* Edited by his Sister. London: Rivingtons, 1885.

'Mr. Pips, His Diary,' London *Punch*, May 5, 1849.

Müller, F. Max: *Auld Lang Syne*. New York: Charles Scribner's Sons, 1898.

Müller, F. Max: *The Life and Letters of the Right Honorable Friedrich Max Müller*. Edited by his Wife. New York: Longmans, Green and Company, 1902.

Niecks, Frederick: *Frederick Chopin as a Man and Musician*. Volume II. London and New York: Novello, Ewer and Company, 1888.

Norlind, Tobias: *Jenny Lind, en minnesbok till hundraårs-dagen*. Stockholm: Wahlström and Wildstrand, 1919.

Owen, Richard: *The Life of Richard Owen*. Two volumes. New York: D. Appleton and Company, 1894.

Paget, Stephen [ed.]: *Henry Scott Holland: Memoir and Letters*. London: John Murray, 1921.

Papin, Theophile: 'Jenny Lind in St. Louis,' *Music*, XIX, November, 1900, 20–34.

Pearce, Charles E.: *Sims Reeves. Fifty Years of Music in England*. London: Stanley Paul and Company, Limited, 1924.

Peel, Ethel [ed.]: *Recollections of Lady Georgiana Peel*. London: John Lane, 1920.

Pickering, Spencer [ed.]: *Memoirs of Anna Maria Wilhelmina Pickering. Together with Extracts from the Journals of her Father, John Spencer Stanhope.* London: Hodder and Stoughton, 1903.

Pollock, Sir Frederick: *Personal Remembrances.* Volume II. London: Macmillan and Company, Limited, 1887.

Redesdale, Lord: *Memories.* Two volumes. London: Hutchinson and Company, n.d.

Reeves, J. Sims: *My Jubilee, or Fifty Years of Artistic Life.* London: The London Music Publishing Company, Limited, 1889.

'Resurrecting Jenny Lind,' *The Literary Digest*, LXVII, October 23, 1920, pp. 30–31. (An account of the Jenny Lind centenary celebration in New York.)

Reumert, Elith: *Hans Andersen the Man.* New York: E. P. Dutton and Company, n.d.

Review of the Performances of Mademoiselle Jenny Lind, During Her Engagement at Her Majesty's Theatre, and Their Influence and Effect upon our National Drama: With a Notice of Her Life. London: J. and L. Dickinson, 1847.

Rockstro, W. S.: *Jenny Lind, A Record and Analysis of the 'Method' of the late Madame Jenny Lind-Goldschmidt.... Together with a Selection of Cadenze, Solfeggi, Abellimenti, &c. in Illustration of Her Vocal Art*, edited by Otto Goldschmidt. London: Novello and Company, Limited, 1894. (Practically reprinted from Holland and Rockstro.)

Rosenberg, C. G.: *Jenny Lind: Her Life, Her Struggles, and Her Triumphs.* New York: Stringer and Townsend, 1850.

Rosenberg, C. G.: *Jenny Lind in America*. New York: Stringer and Townsend, 1851.

Ryan, Thomas: *Recollections of an Old Musician*. New York: E. P. Dutton and Company, 1899.

Sanborn, Alvan F. [ed.]: *Reminiscences of Richard Lathers. Sixty Years of a Busy Life in South Carolina, Massachusetts, and New York*. New York: The Grafton Press, 1907.

Scott, Leonora Cranch: *The Life and Letters of Christopher Pearse Cranch*. Boston: Houghton Mifflin Company, 1917.

Seitz, Don C.: *The James Gordon Bennetts, Father and Son, Proprietors of the New York Herald*. Indianapolis: The Bobbs-Merrill Company, 1928.

Simpson, M. C. M.: *Many Memories of Many People*. London: Edward Arnold, 1898.

Smith, Charles Eastlake [ed.]: *Journals and Correspondence of Lady Eastlake*. Volume II. London: John Murray, 1895.

Smith, John Jay: *Recollections*. Philadelphia: Privately printed, 1892.

Smyth, Albert H.: *Bayard Taylor*. Boston: Houghton Mifflin Company, 1896.

Spångberg, Ernest A.: *The Life of Jenny Lind, A Compilation from Various Sources, in Commemoration of the Centenary of her Birth*. Minneapolis, 1920. (No publisher named.)

St. Helier, Lady (Mary Jeune): *Memories of Fifty Years*. London: Edward Arnold, 1910.

Stowe, Charles Edward: *Life of Harriet Beecher Stowe*. Boston: Houghton Mifflin Company. [^c1889.]

Sullivan, Herbert, and Flower, Newman: *Sir Arthur Sulli-*

van. *His Life, Letters and Diaries.* London: Cassell and Company, Limited, 1927.

Svensk Tidskrift för musik forskning. The issue for August 2, 1920, is devoted to Jenny Lind. It contains a good deal of information in the way of bibliography and a list of portraits.

Symonds, Margaret: *Out of the Past.* London: John Murray, 1925.

Taylor, Marie Hansen, and Scudder, Horace E.: *Life and Letters of Bayard Taylor.* Volume II. Boston: Houghton Mifflin Company. [ᶜ1884.]

Tompkins, Ira Gale: 'Jenny Lind's First Concert in America. Related by an Eye and Ear Witness,' *Music,* x (1896), 145–54.

Trowbridge, John Townsend: *My Own Story, with Recollections of Noted Persons.* Boston: Houghton Mifflin Company. [ᶜ1903.] (This book contains an interesting account of the Boston auction.)

Tuckermann, Henry T.: *Essays Biographical and Critical, or Studies of Character.* Boston: Phillips, Sampson and Company, 1857.

Upton, George P.: *Musical Memories. My Recollections of Celebrities of the Half Century, 1850–1900.* Chicago: A. C. McClurg and Company, 1908.

Upton, George P.: *Theodore Thomas, A Musical Autobiography.* Volume I. Chicago: A. C. McClurg and Company, 1905.

Weigall, Lady Rose [ed.]: *The Correspondence of Priscilla, Countess of Westmorland.* London: John Murray, 1909.

Werner, M. R.: *Barnum.* New York: Harcourt, Brace and Company, 1923.

Westervelt, Leonidas: *The Jenny Lind Medals and Tokens.* (Numismatic Notes and Monographs, No. 5.) New York: The American Numismatic Society, 1921.

Westervelt, Leonidas: 'On the Trail of Jenny Lind,' *Musical Courier*, LXXXVIII, June 12, 1924, pp. 6–7, 47.

Whipple, Henry Benjamin: *Lights and Shadows of a Long Episcopate.* New edition. New York: The Macmillan Company, 1912.

White, Maude Valérie: *Friends and Memories.* London: Edward Arnold, 1914.

Wilkens, C. A.: *Jenny Lind.* Geneva: J. H. Jeheber, n.d.

Willis, N. Parker: *Famous Persons and Places.* Auburn and Rochester: Alden and Beardsley, 1855.

Willis, N. Parker: *Hurry-graphs; or Sketches of Scenery, Celebrities, and Society, Taken from Life.* Auburn and Rochester: Alden, Beardsley and Company, 1853.

Willis, N. Parker: *Memoranda of the Life of Jenny Lind.* Philadelphia: Robert E. Peterson, 1851.

REFERENCES

REFERENCES

Chapter I: The Legend

1. Field, p. 220.
2. Ryan, p. 136.
3. Longfellow, ii, 197.
4. Rosenberg, *Jenny Lind in America*, p. 45.
5. *Ibid.*, p. 216 ff.
6. Upton, *Musical Memories*, p. 23.
7. Barnum, p. 333.
8. Upton, *Musical Memories*, p. 21.
9. Rosenberg, *Jenny Lind in America*, p. 57.
10. Upton, *Musical Memories*, p. 21.
11. Mrs. Maude, p. 98.
12. Rosenberg, *Jenny Lind in America*, p. 57.
13. Kellogg, p. 5.
14. Emerson, viii, 129, 247.
15. Upton, *Musical Memories*, p. 19.
16. Rosenberg, *Jenny Lind in America*, p. 84.
17. *Ibid.*, pp. 19–20, 23, 45.
18. Willis, *Memo.*, p. 95.
19. *Ibid.*, p. 185.
20. For a good many of the details in this section, I am indebted to Mr. M. R. Werner's lively account of the American reception in his *Barnum*. Mr. Werner did an immense amount of work on this phase of Jenny Lind's career, and I have shamelessly entered into the inheritance. Where no other authority is cited in this first section of Chapter I, I am generally relying on Mr. Werner.

21. Congdon, p. 199.
22. Mrs. Maude, p. 98.
23. Foster, p. 58.
24. Rosenberg, *Jenny Lind*, p. 62.
25. Spångberg, p. 40.
26. Rosenberg, *Jenny Lind*, p. 55.
27. See bibliography.
28. 'Lost Road,' *Yale Review*, XIX (1929), 134–47.
29. Haven and Russell, pp. 130–31.
30. In making this outline of Jenny Lind's career, I have followed Holland and Rockstro as far as it goes; thereafter I have relied generally on Mrs. Maude.

Chapter II: The Artist

1. Curtis, p. 147.
2. Werner, p. 188.
3. Barnum, p. 341.
4. *Ibid.*, p. 351.
5. Winifred Ponder, *Clara Butt, Her Life Story* (London, George G. Harrap, 1928), p. 131.
6. *New Republic*, XI (1917), 280–81.
7. Werner, p. 168.
8. Longfellow, II, 179.
9. Benson and Esher, II, 144.
10. Macready, II, 367.
11. Karasowski, II, 347.
12. Holland and Rockstro, I, 5.
13. Werner, p. 132.
14. Carlyle, II, 64. Cf. Werner, pp. 170–71.

15. Werner, p. 132.
16. Werner, p. 168.
17. Horace Taubel, *With Whitman in Camden*, I, 335, 456. (Quoted by Gamaliel Bradford, in his portrait of Edwin Booth, *As God Made Them*, Boston, Houghton Mifflin Company, 1929, pp. 177–78.)
18. Ellis, I, 40.
19. Macpherson, p. 263.
20. Chorley, pp. 198–99.
21. A. Coleridge, p. 102.
22. Chorley, p. 78.
23. *Scribner's Monthly*, XXII, 124.
24. Longfellow, II, 220–21.
25. Holland and Rockstro, I, 353–54.
26. Macready, II, 369.
27. *Famous Persons*, p. 396.
28. Such an analysis has been made in Holland and Rockstro, Book VIII, ch. II. See also 'Rockstro' in the bibliography.
29. *Scribner's Monthly*, XXII, 126.
30. Mrs. Maude, p. 129.
31. The same situation prevails in motion picture criticism, where there is indeed an added difficulty in the absence of an adequate vocabulary. See Gilbert Seldes's interesting statement of the resemblances between motion pictures and music, in *The Movies and the Talkies* (Philadelphia, J. B. Lippincott Company, 1929).
32. For the argument and the illustration in the latter half of this paragraph, I am indebted to a suggestion made by my friend and former teacher, the late

Professor Albert H. Tolman, of the University of Chicago.

33. *Scribner's Magazine*, XLVII, 429–30.
34. Appy, *Century*, XXXII, 554, 556.
35. Mrs. Maude, p. 133.
36. Brown, *J. A. Symonds*, I, 198.
37. Lodge, pp. 153–54.
38. Holland and Rockstro, I, 16.
39. *Ibid.*, II, 389. Cf. Litzmann, I, 468.
40. Moscheles, *Life*, II, 283.
41. Cavendish, II, 168.
42. Weigall, p. 192.
43. *Musical Quarterly*, III (1917), 548–51.
44. Mackinlay, pp. 148, 288.
45. Kellogg, p. 6.
46. Brown, *J. A. Symonds*, I, 207.
47. Holland and Rockstro, II, 300–01.
48. *Ibid.*, I, 115–16.
49. *Scribner's Monthly*, XXII, 132. The sentence, which is quoted from memory, has distinctly a copy-book ring. But doubtless it reproduces accurately enough the *substance* of what Jenny Lind said.
50. Chorley, pp. 196–97. Cf. Holland and Rockstro, I, 431.
51. A. Coleridge, p. 97.
52. Hallé, p. 115.
53. *Century*, XXXII, 556.
54. Smyth, pp. 82–83.
55. Rosenberg, *Jenny Lind in America*, p. 94.
56. Norlind, p. 213.
57. Mrs. Maude, pp. 93–94.

58. Frederick H. Martens, *The Art of the Prima Donna* (New York, D. Appleton and Company, 1923), p. 91.

59. Brown, *J. A. Symonds*, I, 204.

60. Chorley, p. 198.

61. *Musical Memories*, p. 23.

62. *Scribner's Magazine*, XLVII, 429–30.

63. Higginson, *T. W. Higginson*, pp. 99–100.

64. *Century*, XXXII, 556.

65. Barnum, p. 368; Werner, pp. 179, 182–83.

66. Ganz, p. 72.

67. Holland and Rockstro, II, 96.

68. 'The Story of My Life,' Third article, *Photoplay Magazine*, April, 1919, pp. 53–54.

69. Holland and Rockstro, II, 70.

70. Chorley, p. 198.

71. *Scribner's Monthly*, XXII, 126.

72. Reeves, p. 98; Pearce, pp. 116–22. H. E. Krehbiel, *How to Listen to Music* (New York, Charles Scribner's Sons, 1897), pp. 243–44, and again in his article in the *New York Tribune*, October 10, 1920, declares that when Jenny Lind sang Alice in *Roberto*, she caused the rôle of Isabella to be eliminated because she wished to be the only woman among the principal characters of the opera. I have been unable to find any authority for this statement.

73. Norlind, p. 144.

74. Holland and Rockstro, I, 178.

75. *Ibid.*, I, 303–04.

76. *The Art of Acting* (New York, Publications of the Dramatic Museum of Columbia University, 1926).

There is a very sane and well-balanced discussion of this whole question of the relation between an actor's emotions and his work in the chapter 'How Not To Act,' in DeWolf Hopper's reminiscences, *Once A Clown, Always A Clown* (Boston, Little, Brown and Company, 1927).

77. Norlind, p. 213.
78. Holland and Rockstro, II, 173.
79. *Ibid.*, I, 273–74, 321, 424.
80. *Ibid.*, I, 138.
81. *Ibid.*, I, 125–26.
82. *Ibid.*, I, 390.
83. Willis, *Memo.*, p. 198.
84. Holland and Rockstro, I, 395.
85. *Ibid.*, I, 316.
86. *Ibid.*, II, 84.
87. *Ibid.*, II, 63.
88. *Ibid.*, I, 276.
89. *Ibid.*, I, 293.
90. *Ibid.*, I, 246.
91. *Ibid.*, II, 64–65.
92. *Ibid.*, I, 135.
93. Andersen, p. 208.
94. Holland and Rockstro, I, 208.
95. Norlind, p. 69.
96. Holland and Rockstro, I, 124.
97. *Ibid.*, I, 138.
98. *Ibid.*, I, 136.
99. *Ibid.*, I, 138.
100. *Ibid.*, I, 125.
101. *Ibid.*, II, 85.

102. *Loc. cit.*
103. *Ibid.*, I, 126. Cf. I, 320.
104. *Ibid.*, II, 445–47.
105. *Ibid.*, II, 6.
106. *Ibid.*, I, 317.
107. *Musical Quarterly*, III, 518.
108. Holland and Rockstro, I, 126.
109. *Ibid.*, II, 34.
110. *Ibid.*, I, 150.
111. *Ibid.*, II, 292.
112. *Ibid.*, I, 276–77.
113. Werner, pp. 129–30.
114. Marie Bashkirtseff, *The Journal of a Young Artist, 1860–1884.* Translated by Mary J. Serrano. New edition (New York, E. P. Dutton and Company, 1919), Preface.
115. Holland and Rockstro, I, 163.
116. *Ibid.*, I, 170.
117. *Ibid.*, I, 193.

Chapter III: The Woman

1. Foreword to Lillie Langtry, *The Days I Knew* (New York, George H. Doran Company, 1925).
2. Holland and Rockstro, II, 446.
3. Norlind, p. 108.
4. Bournonville, p. 298.
5. Holland and Rockstro, I, 198.
6. Locker-Lampson, p. 166.
7. Hegermann-Lindencrone, p. 84.
8. Brown, *J. A. Symonds*, I, 198, 202.
9. Mrs. Maude, p. 208.

10. Bournonville, p. 299.
11. Holland and Rockstro, I, 85.
12. Brown, *J. A. Symonds*, I, 201.
13. Hegermann-Lindencrone, pp. 85–86.
14. *Ibid.*, p. 84.
15. Longfellow, II, 197.
16. Mozley, p. 196.
17. *Baltimore Sun*, Sept. 28, 1920. (In *Press Books*.)
18. Haweis, *Contemporary Review*, LIX, 908.
19. Ellsworth, *A Golden Age of Authors* (Boston, Houghton Mifflin Company, 1919), p. 220.
20. Broughton, VI, 193.
21. Brown, *J. A. Symonds*, I, 201.
22. *Ibid.*, I, 207.
23. *Ibid.*, I, 202.
24. Hoffman, *Scribner's Magazine*, XLVII, 431.
25. Norlind, p. 216. Cf. Holland, *Living Age*, CLXXV, 751–57.
26. Holland and Rockstro, I, 29–30.
27. *Musical Quarterly*, III, 548.
28. Holland and Rockstro, I, 83–84.
29. *Ibid.*, I, 73.
30. *Ibid.*, I, 349.
31. Brown, *J. A. Symonds*, I, 209.
32. Holland and Rockstro, I, 179–80; 350.
33. Brown, *J. A. Symonds*, I, 208.
34. See her letter to Mrs. Stowe, in C. E. Stowe, pp. 183–84.
35. Pollock, II, 114.
36. Brown, *J. A. Symonds*, I, 209.
37. *Ibid.*, I, 207.

38. Holland and Rockstro, I, 136, 170.
39. Mrs. Maude, p. 207.
40. Brown, *J. A. Symonds*, I, 200.
41. Barnum, p. 349. I suppose any statement which rests on Barnum's testimony alone should be taken with a grain of salt.
42. Holland and Rockstro, II, 19.
43. Hoffman, *Scribner's Magazine*, XLVII, 432.
44. Holland and Rockstro, II, 418.
45. *Ibid.*, I, 61; cf. I, 38.
46. *Ibid.*, II, 157.
47. *Musical Quarterly*, III, 548.
48. Norlind, p. 136.
49. Holland and Rockstro, II, 348.
50. *Ibid.*, II, 319.
51. *Ibid.*, II, 306.
52. Reeves, pp. 203–04.
53. Mrs. Maude, p. 128. Cf. also Lehmann, pp. 32–33; Hegermann-Lindencrone, p. 85.
54. Andersen, p. 207.
55. Erskine, p. 249.
56. Broughton, VI, 190.
57. Willis, *Famous Places*, p. 426.
58. Holland, *Living Age*, CLXXV, 755.
59. Werner, p. 175. Cf. cartoon in Meighan.
60. Greeley, p. 237.
61. Barnum, p. 363.
62. *Ibid.*, pp. 362–63.
63. Holland and Rockstro, II, 421.
64. Brown, *J. A. Symonds*, I, 202.
65. Litzmann, I, 470.

66. Barnum, p. 332.
67. Holland and Rockstro, I, 332; Haweis, *Contemporary Review*, LIX, 907.
68. Hegermann-Lindencrone, p. 85; Rosenberg, *Jenny Lind in America*, pp. 29–30 — an instance where her sense of humour got the better of her indignation. Cf. the story of the railway porter, in Mrs. Maude, p. 215.
69. Cf. S. Coleridge, p. 98.
70. A. Coleridge, pp. 106–07.
71. St. Helier, p. 194.
72. Simpson, pp. 92–93.
73. Barnum, p. 356.
74. Simpson, p. 92.
75. Holland, *Living Age*, CLXXV, 754.
76. Pollock, II, 114.
77. Elmblad, p. 43.
78. Norlind, p. 96.
79. Holland and Rockstro, II, 86. Cf. II, 41.
80. *Ibid.*, I, 87.
81. Ecclesiastes, VII, 16 and VII, 6.
82. Holland and Rockstro, I, 333.
83. Barnum, p. 356.
84. Mrs. Maude, p. 27.
85. Peele, pp. 146–47.
86. McNeill, *Century*, XXIII, 208.
87. Holland, *Living Age*, CLXXV, 754.
88. Andersen, p. 296.
89. Willis, *Memo.*, pp. 36–37.
90. Holland and Rockstro, I, 78.
91. Brown, *J. A. Symonds*, I, 216.

92. Mrs. Maude, p. 213; cf. J. J. Smith, p. 156.
93. Bournonville, pp. 300–01.
94. Reeves, p. 203.
95. Brown, *J. A. Symonds*, I, 206.
96. A. Coleridge, p. 106.
97. Holland and Rockstro, II, 433.
98. Holland, *Living Age*, CLXXV, 754.
99. Barnum, p. 357.
100. Holland and Rockstro, II, 317.
101. Marsh, *New England Magazine*, VI, 399.
102. A. Coleridge, p. 104. Cf. Greenwood, p. 5, an account of Jenny Lind's kindness to seasick fellow-passengers.
103. Holland and Rockstro, II, 202.
104. Cook, I, 232.
105. Brown, *J. A. Symonds*, I, 208.
106. *Ibid.*, I, 215.
107. Macready, II, 365.
108. Holland and Rockstro, I, 34.
109. Reeves, pp. 204–05.
110. Holland, *Living Age*, CLXXV, 754.
111. Holland and Rockstro, II, 350.
112. Willis, *Famous Places*, p. 430.
113. Holland and Rockstro, II, 377; cf. *Ibid.*, II, 27; Marsh, *New England Magazine*, VI, 399; Hamilton, p. 62.
114. Symonds, p. 148.
115. Appy, *Century*, XXXII, 554.
116. Hoffman, *Scribner's Magazine*, XLVII, 428–29.
117. Benedict, *Scribner's Monthly*, XXII, 120.
118. Field, p. 219; cf. Werner, p. 191.

119. Barnum, p. 353.
120. Holland and Rockstro, II, 335.
121. *Ibid.*, II, 204, 340.
122. *Ibid.*, II, 344–45; Werner, pp. 136–37.
123. Holland and Rockstro, I, 322.
124. Willis, *Famous Persons*, pp. 430–31; Hoffman, *Scribner's Magazine*, XLVII, 430; Werner, p. 191.
125. Norlind, p. 89, p. 183.
126. Frothingham, p. 312.
127. Mrs. Maude, p. 188.
128. *Ibid.*, p. 190.
129. Cf. Werner, pp. 185–86, note; Cyril Maude, pp. 30–32.
130. Marsh, *New England Magazine*, VI, 399.
131. Mrs. Maude, p. 207.
132. Hoffman, *Scribner's Magazine*, XLVII, 432.
133. Bickley, p. 290.
134. Westervelt, *Musical Courier*, June 12, 1924.
135. Field, p. 219.
136. Barnum, p. 384.
137. *Ibid.*, p. 387.
138. Holland and Rockstro, II, 370. Probably the most illustrious beneficiary of Miss Lind's bounty was Sir Arthur Sullivan. (Cf. Sullivan and Flower.) Those who find her austerity too unbearable may possibly derive some comfort from the reflection that the gay and precious talent to which we owe the overture to *Pinafore* and the love-duet from *Iolanthe* was indebted to her for its development. Jenny Lind never lost her interest in Sullivan's career.
139. Field, p. 220.

140. Barnum, p. 348.
141. Rosenberg, *Jenny Lind*, p. 30.
142. *Ibid.*, p. 53.
143. Holland and Rockstro, i, 218.
144. Hegermann-Lindencrone, p. 86.
145. Barnum, p. 378.

Chapter IV: The Artist, The Woman, and God

1. Holland, *Living Age*, CLXXV, 754. Cf. Brown, *Letters*, p. 202.
2. Holland and Rockstro, i, 25.
3. *Ibid.*, ii, 201.
4. Hoffman, *Scribner's Magazine*, XLVII, 431.
5. Holland and Rockstro, ii, 194.
6. Niecks, ii, 284.
7. Bickley, p. 84. Miss Farrar writes me that Ödman, who in his youth had sung with Jenny Lind, and who, when he was past sixty, sang opposite Miss Farrar in Stockholm, 'had rather harsh things to say of her [Jenny's] petty jealousy among comrades, and an air of false piety that evidently disturbed the volatile ones in the métier.'
8. White, p. 300.
9. Litzmann, ii, 283.
10. Cook, i, 231–32.
11. A. Coleridge, p. 110.
12. Lehmann, p. 33.
13. Rosenberg, *Jenny Lind in America*, p. 37.
14. Holland and Rockstro, ii, 396.
15. *Ibid.*, ii, 433. Cf. i, 138–39, 180; ii, 421.
16. Brown, *J. A. Symonds*, i, 216.

17. Holland, *Living Age*, CLXXV, 753.
18. *Ibid.*, 756.
19. *Ibid.*, 755–56.
20. Holland and Rockstro, II, 164.
21. *Geraldine Farrar, The Story of an American Singer* (Boston, Houghton Mifflin Company, 1916), p. 1.
22. Holland and Rockstro, II, 6.
23. Spångberg, pp. 44–45.
24. *Ibid.*, p. 33.
25. *Lives of Good and Great Women*, p. 273. It should be noted that this quotation is somewhat unauthenticated appearing, so far as I am aware, only in this anonymous book. But the point seems characteristic.
26. *Portraits of American Women* (Boston, Houghton Mifflin Company, 1919) pp. 197–225.
27. *D. L. Moody, A Worker in Souls* (New York, George H. Doran Company, 1927).
28. *Life and I, An Autobiography of Humanity* (Boston, Houghton Mifflin Company, 1928).
29. Andersen, p. 401.
30. Werner, p. 131; cf. p. 197.
31. Bournonville, pp. 300–01.
32. Geraldine Farrar, 'Coming Back and Looking Back,' *Saturday Evening Post*, CC, April 14, 1928, pp. 18–19, 122, 125, 128.
33. Holland and Rockstro, II, 437.
34. *Ibid.*, I, 225.
35. *Ibid.*, II, 438.
36. Brown, *J. A. Symonds*, I, 217.
37. Holland and Rockstro, I, 365.

38. Holland and Rockstro, I, 246.
39. Andersen, p. 211.
40. *Review*, p. 23.
41. Holland and Rockstro, I, 306.
42. Rosenberg, *Jenny Lind*, pp. 43–44.
43. Charles Edward Russell, *Julia Marlowe — Her Life and Art* (New York, D. Appleton and Company, 1926), pp. 365–66.
44. *Mont-Saint-Michel and Chartres* (Boston, Houghton Mifflin Company, 1904), pp. 196–97.
45. *The Wallet of Time* (New York, Moffat, Yard and Company, 1913), I, 371–72.
46. *Œdipus or Pollyanna* (Seattle, University of Washington Book Store, 1927), p. 23.
47. *The Wallet of Time*, II, 8–10.
48. Holland and Rockstro, II, 352.
49. Abbott, p. 29.
50. Werner, p. 167.
51. Hoffman, *Scribner's Magazine*, XLVII, 430. I am beginning to wonder whether Daniel Webster did not make something of a habit of bowing to Jenny Lind. Here he is bowing after hearing 'I Know That My Redeemer Liveth'; there is record elsewhere of his bowing after a Swedish folk-song; and in Foote's *Casket of Reminiscences*, pp. 9–11, there is an exceedingly amusing story of a series of bows he directed toward her after her singing of 'The Star-Spangled Banner.' When she had once been thus honored, 'The amiable and accomplished recipient of a homage as unexpected as it must have been gratifying, manifested something of a graceful and

blushing embarrassment, but courtesied notwith-standing most profoundly in response, upon which the assembled multitude gave vent to their delight in most vociferous applause. A second bow was administered, with precisely similar accompani-ments. A third one was tendered, when the "Swed-ish Nightingale," as she was called, incontinently took wing and became invisible to our fond and ad-miring eyes, perchance forever.' This item comes to my attention through the courtesy of Mr. W. C. Bayles, of Seattle.

52. Mrs. Maude, p. 151. Lyman Abbott suggests this also by printing *know* in italics.

53. *Scribner's Magazine*, XLVII, 430.

54. *Century*, XXXII, 556.

55. Quoted in *The Literary Digest*, LXVII, October 23, 1920, p. 30.

INDEX

INDEX

countries, 110–11; attitude towards society, 112–16; indifference to eating and drinking, 116–17; social success complicated by her fame, 117; anecdotes illustrating her austerity, 117–20; her idealism and bad temper, 120–21; her tendency toward melancholy, 121–23; her sense of humour, 123–24; her recreations, 125; as a hostess, 125–26; at children's parties, 126; at a New Year's party, 126; her devotion to friends, 127–28; her choice of friends, 128–29; relations with her mother, 129–30; what she expected of her friends, 131–32; her failures in friendship, 131; her attitude towards love and marriage, 132–33; her children, 133–34; early admirers, 134; Mendelssohn, 134; her love affair with Julius Günther, 135; with Claudius Harris, 135–38; her marriage to Otto Goldschmidt, 138–42; her attitude towards money, 142–44; her charities, 144–49.

Her primary interest in religion, 153; awakening of her religious feeling, 153–54; her innate spirituality, 154–

55; narrower aspects of her religion, 155–57; her austerity and pietism, 157–59; her dislike of Catholicism, 159–61; her growth in spiritual grace, 161; her religious doubts and difficulties, 161–63; her absolute loyalty, 163; interweaving of her religion and her career, 164; her sense of divine leadership, 164–65; was she ambitious for herself? 165–67; the charge that her religion destroyed her career considered, 167–68; why did she leave the theater? 168–70; what her religion contributed to her art, 170 ff.; the note of spiritual exaltation in her work, 175 ff.; her singing in oratorio, 183–85; she conquered the world and threw it away for God, 185–86.

Index

Index